DITCH YOUR INNER CRITIC AT WORK

EVIDENCE-BASED STRATEGIES TO THRIVE IN YOUR CAREER

SUSAN PEPPERCORN

Dover, Massachusetts

Copyright © 2017 by Susan Peppercorn

All rights reserved. No part of this book may be used or reproduced in any manner without written permission from the author.

Names and identifying details have been changed to protect the privacy of individuals.

www.positiveworkplacepartners.com

Published 2017

Cover design by Sherwin Soy
Edited by Robin Madell

Library of Congress Control Number: 2017955799

ISBN: 978-0-9994536-1-2
eISBN: 978-0-9994536-0-5

1. Business, 2. Career development, 3. Success, 4. Success in business,
5. Positive psychology, 6. Happiness

Table of Contents

Introduction

Have you reached a point in your career where regardless of your level of external success, you feel stagnant, unmotivated, and empty inside? Did the education you pursued fail to lead you to work satisfaction and fulfillment? Do you find yourself held hostage by critical inner voices that tell you nothing you do is good enough? If you answered yes to any of these questions, then this book is for you.

The topic of work satisfaction is a very personal one to me. In all of my previous jobs, though I was successful by conventional standards, I was accompanied by an ever-present inner critic that was loud and, at times, debilitating. It never dawned on me that work and happiness could be synonymous. Although I read one self-help book after another in an attempt to gain relief, none seemed to offer the lasting results I craved.

Five years ago, eager to find relevant solutions to share with my coaching clients, I embarked on a personal study of positive psychology, the branch of social science that examines how and why people thrive. Until the late 1990s, the focus of psychology had been on treating dysfunction. But positive psychology, through its rigorous scientific research, opened a door to practical strategies that anyone can implement who wants to live a fuller, happier life. It was through the analysis of these findings that I realized this modality offers endless opportunities for people to improve their careers.

Study after study has shown that most workers do not feel engaged in their work. This indifference costs billions of dollars in sick days and low productivity. More importantly from an individual perspective, disengagement takes a huge toll on people's well-being when they feel stuck in jobs they dislike, or paralyzed by the "I'm not enough" mindset.

Earlier in my career, this was definitely true for me. For far too long, I stayed in a job that drained rather than fulfilled me. Despite the fact that I received plenty of positive feedback in my role, Monday morning anxiety attacks became a regular occurrence—as did the daily feeling of dread that surged through me as I prepared to endure a job I didn't enjoy and wasn't my calling. It took me years to discover and embark on a career that I love, and I came upon it more through happenstance than planning.

You need not make the same mistakes that I did, and I've written this book to show you how to avoid them. One thing I've learned is that each of us possesses an inner drive to find meaning and purpose in our work. When you're aware of this, discovering a route to finding passion and significance in your career need not be a random process—on the contrary, it can be very intentional. This book reveals how to find a deep level of satisfaction in your career that's based on your own image of success and happiness, not someone else's.

My personal career path resulted from a series of decisions that were not particularly well contemplated or planned. Graduating with two degrees in musical performance, I learned early on that I would need to pivot into another field in order to support myself. Only a rarified few can make it as a professional musician, and I was not one of them. After taking a job as a music teacher shortly after graduation, I quickly realized that it wasn't for me, and two years later entered the high-tech industry in sales.

The first few years in my new role were very exciting, and the fast-growing company I had joined offered many opportunities for advancement. I was the first female salesperson hired, and the youngest to be promoted to sales manager. At the age of 26, I was put in charge of managing a team responsible for a multimillion-dollar relationship with a major bank in New York City—a challenging role, to say the least. As we grew the business, I was rewarded with trips to many wonderful destinations including the South of France, Australia, and Mexico.

Unfortunately, the good life grew increasingly unsatisfactory, and as more challenges arose in my position, I realized that I was burning out. As the job morphed from dream to nightmare, I found myself in a constant state of worry and apprehension. This was exacerbated by a tough inner critic that chimed in to tell me I wasn't up to the task. As such, I was held hostage by my negative thoughts, and the resulting stress crushed my energy and soul. On top of dealing with my lack of confidence, the role was a terrible fit for my interests and values; technology wasn't particularly interesting to me, and once the initial excitement of the perks faded, hawking computer hardware for a living began to feel meaningless. Yet as much as I wanted to make a change, I didn't know what alternatives existed. I felt handcuffed by the generous compensation, as well as by my mindset that convinced me I was stuck where I was. Believing there were no better options, I stayed in the job even though everything inside me wanted to leave.

Fast forward 15 years: the company I worked for was purchased, and I finally had no choice but to do something different. Though I was relieved to leave the technology world behind, I felt frightened about what was to come since I had not allowed myself the opportunity to explore other possibilities.

As I thought about what I might do next, I realized that I wanted to work closer to home. The recognition of this priority and value of work-life balance helped guide me toward potential opportunities, since it narrowed the universe of options and helped me hone in on the right ballpark. I soon learned of an interesting position at a local college five minutes away that required someone with a strong business development background. That was me! One thing led to another, and before long, I was recruited to another university where I started coaching students. It was in this role that a light bulb went on: this is what I wanted to do! Since then, I have devoted myself to coaching people in career transition. It's a vocation that's the right fit for my interests, values, and skills, and thus brings me a high degree of satisfaction and fulfillment. In a nutshell, my job makes me happy—and I want you to be able to feel the same thing.

By the time you're done reading this book, you'll have all the tools you need to be able to move from just surviving to totally thriving in your career. No matter what types of challenges are keeping you stuck, you'll understand how to combat them. Whether it's a relentless inner critic that you need to push back on, a bent toward perfectionism that needs to be tempered, or hidden biases keeping you from recognizing and embracing work you find meaningful, this book will equip you to address your stumbling blocks and start making needed changes.

As a preview of what's to come, the book is divided into three parts: Recognize, Redefine, and Re-engage. Within each section, the chapters contain exercises to help you clarify your thinking and aspirations while measuring where you are versus where you want to be.

In Part 1, Recognize, you'll learn that the first step in making a thoughtful career change is first to recognize the assumptions and thoughts that are holding you back. Without the awareness of how your inner critic and self-limiting beliefs are hurting you, the decisions you make will likely be based on others' expectations rather than on your authentic self. In this section, I'll share what scientists have learned about happiness—what leads to it and what doesn't—and then offer strategies for overcoming negative self-talk.

In Part 2, Redefine, you'll learn how to see yourself through the lens of your capabilities and most influential experiences. Building on the foundation of what psychologists have determined are the pillars of career satisfaction—strengths, values, and interests—you'll finally be able to question long-held, limiting convictions and see yourself in a more accepting light.

In Part 3, Re-engage, we'll get down to brass tacks with strategies for moving forward. You'll learn how to experience flow, harness your resources, become more accepting of perceived failures, and starting taking needed action toward a more meaningful, and happier, work life.

Most of us will have many different jobs and make at least one major career shift in our lifetime. Knowing how to navigate not only the tactical but also the emotional aspects of these changes will increase your chances of staying grounded and optimistic through transition phases. My hope for you on your journey is the same one I share with my coaching clients: that through this process, you come to see that seeking job satisfaction, meaningful work, and even happiness in your career are all achievable goals—and that your thinking and actions can significantly impact the outcome. By embracing and investing in your true self, you'll discover that you indeed have the power to create a future that is both energizing and rewarding.

Part One

RECOGNIZE

ONE

Getting to Know Your Inner Critic

Life does not consist mainly, or even largely, of facts or happenings. It consists mainly of the storm of thoughts that is forever flowing through one's head.

—Mark Twain

Do you have an inner critic? If so, you're not alone. No matter how seemingly successful many of us are at work or in our personal life, it can be difficult to avoid an internal voice of self-doubt and self-admonishment. At its most basic level, this is because from a very young age, we develop belief systems about ourselves based on feedback and expectations expressed by people we think know more than we do: parents, teachers, friends, peers, and even acquaintances.

This may seem innocent enough—perhaps in some cases they *do* know more than you do. But when you buy into others' belief systems without questioning their fit in your own life, you essentially allow someone else to rent space in your head. If that renter is frequently negative and critical, the results are not very pleasant and can lead you to experience emotional distress as your inner critic repeats what an outside critic has said about you.

If you listen too closely to your inner critic, this voice can lead you astray in a number of arenas, including your career. The problem starts when you fall into the trap of looking outward to the expectations of others instead of looking inward, in essence giving up an independent, concrete sense of self and control over your own destiny. In responding to others' expectations of you rather than your own, it's easy to lose sight of your own vision and priorities. Where you are today in your career—what you do for a living and how you feel about it—has close ties to what others have told you about who you should be and whether you have taken them at their word.

THE CULPRIT BEHIND THE CRITIC: PERFECTIONISM

In my work as a career and life coach, I've seen one particularly damaging outcome of tuning in too often to an inner critic. I've worked with many clients whose goal was to pinpoint the ideal role for themselves, or the "perfect" job rather than seeking the right job for their particular talents, skills, and career level. This type of perfectionistic thinking can force you into an "all-or-nothing" trap, where you feel pigeonholed into sticking with the status quo unless you can find an idealized version of what you think you should be doing with your life.

All-or-nothing thinking is the essence of perfectionism. While our culture often considers striving for perfection desirable, the reality is that perfectionism is self-defeating and self-destructive simply because it creates an unattainable goal while blocking you from what you could effectively achieve in reality.

What's at the root of perfectionistic thought patterns? For many people, trying to control what other people think about them becomes a real monkey on their back (or in their head, as the case may be). You may want to appear as a "perfect person" to others, but since perfection is an impossible goal, this becomes a losing battle that misdirects your energy. This toxic combination of all-or-nothing thinking and trying to control others' perception of you creates the perfect storm that leads many intelligent people to make bad career choices. Before reading on, try Exercise A below to determine where you currently fall on the perfectionism spectrum.

EXERCISE A: SUFFER-SACRIFICE ASSESSMENT

Are you so accustomed to your inner critic that you think it's normal to live with the constant mental chatter of stress, worry, and negativity in your head? Remember, if your definition of success was shaped by the norms you grew up with and those values differ from your own, being self-critical may be the only way you know how to be.

The following exercise is designed to help you determine where you fall on the spectrum relating to the specific perfectionistic tendencies of suffering and sacrifice. For each question, pick the answer that most closely corresponds to how you feel most of the time. Then read the information below the quiz to see if you're a full-fledged perfectionist or have at least some common attributes of perfectionists.

1. People tell me that I have unrealistic expectations.
   a. Frequently
   b. Sometimes
   c. Rarely
   d. Never

2. I tend to judge myself by how much I accomplish.
   a. Frequently
   b. Sometimes
   c. Rarely
   d. Never

3. I miss out on enjoyable events because I have too much work to do.
    a. Frequently
    b. Sometimes
    c. Rarely
    d. Never

4. When I make a mistake, I tend to replay what I did wrong over and over instead of thinking about what I did well.
    a. Frequently
    b. Sometimes
    c. Rarely
    d. Never

5. I minimize my accomplishments.
    a. Frequently
    b. Sometimes
    c. Rarely
    d. Never

6. When I achieve a goal, I enjoy the victory only for a short time before going on to the next project.
    a. Frequently
    b. Sometimes
    c. Rarely
    d. Never

7. I have trouble making decisions.
    a. Frequently
    b. Sometimes
    c. Rarely
    d. Never

8. I set demanding standards for myself and others.
   a. Frequently
   b. Sometimes
   c. Rarely
   d. Never

9. It takes me a long time to bounce back from failure.
   a. Frequently
   b. Sometimes
   c. Rarely
   d. Never

10. I have trouble saying no to my boss because I don't want to let him/her down.
    a. Frequently
    b. Sometimes
    c. Rarely
    d. Never

If you chose "Frequently" for six or more of your answers, you may be limiting yourself and your career because of your purist leanings. If you responded mostly with "Sometimes" or chose "Frequently" to just a few of the questions, you may tend toward being self-critical in some aspects of your life but not others. You can benefit from the strategies in this book even if you aren't a full-blown perfectionist. If you checked the majority of the questions "Rarely" or "Never," keep up the great work! While you may not be battling a strong inner critic in your mind, it's still important to stay on top of how you view success and accomplishment. Even if you're someone who clicks into perfectionist thought patterns only when you feel the situation truly calls for it, you can learn how to maintain your healthy mindset by reading on.

HOW PERFECTIONISM CAN HIJACK YOUR CAREER

Richard, the CEO of a successful biotech startup, consulted with me recently about his future career path. Having just turned 50, he was concerned that he would become unemployable in a decade. After learning that Richard's career had included numerous accomplishments at a large medical device company followed by leading four startups, I asked him why he thought his career options would be limited in the future. His response floored me. He said that because he did not graduate from an Ivy League school, he believed that the venture capital community (made up primarily of Ivy League graduates) would shun him.

I asked Richard, "Given that your educational pedigree hasn't held you back previously, why would it in the future?" It seemed clear to me that this successful C-level executive was destined to continue along his upward trajectory. Yet I can tell you from my vantage point as a career coach working with accomplished professionals, I repeatedly see this pattern of undeserved self-criticism. Like Richard, many people share a preoccupation with their weaknesses (whether or not they are even true), and at the same time fail to recognize their strengths.

It's that all-or-nothing thinking again—and believe me, if you listen to its message, it can lead you astray professionally. For example, imagine if Richard had believed his inner critic initially, assuming at the start of his career that his lack of a degree from a certain school meant that he could never succeed at a high level in business. Had he heeded his inner critic's conviction that only Ivy League graduates would be accepted into the business community, Richard might never have joined the large medical device company that kicked off his career climb, eventually leading him to head four startups and ultimately become chief executive of a profitable biotech firm.

If Richard continues to think perfectionistically about his future career prospects—listening to his inner critic's faulty rationale about the limitations that he imagines he will face based on his past choices rather than seeing the success he has achieved to date—then he will sabotage his chances for career growth. By worrying too much about others' possible (though unlikely) negative perception about where he obtained his university degree, Richard could keep himself from opportunities that would otherwise arise simply by moving forward in the direction that had already brought him significant success.

At this juncture, it's important to note that self-awareness and self-assessment in general are not the problem—far from it. When used fairly to examine your full range of both skills and limitations, such "you-centered" analysis can help you focus on understanding the capabilities you need to move ahead in your career. But when you use self-assessment only to critique and fault-find, failing to consider your strengths and accomplishments as well, then it becomes harmful, not helpful. To continue your own healthy self-assessment, try the following exercise, which will help you identify specific ways that self-criticism may be keeping you from moving ahead in your career.

EXERCISE B:
ARE YOU HOLDING YOURSELF BACK FROM SUCCESS?

Anticipating that failure is just around the corner—or that you might be uncovered as a fraud at any minute—takes a toll on your well-being. Holding yourself and others to unrealistically high standards keeps you from pursuing career opportunities, hurts your relationships, drains your energy, and prevents you from enjoying life to the fullest.

Have you gotten so used to your high level of expectations that you don't stop to question your automatic negative thinking and behavior? The statements below will help you understand if it's time to start questioning the assumptions you've been making about yourself and your career.

9

Answer True or False to the following questions:

1. I haven't applied for—or have turned down—opportunities for promotion or career advancement if I didn't feel 100% ready for them. _____

2. I often work later than my peers. _____

3. I frequently feel tired at work. _____

4. I don't like to delegate to others because if I do the work myself, it will get done the right way. _____

5. When things don't go my way, I ask myself what I did wrong. _____

6. I measure my success largely by comparing my progress to the advancement of my peers and former classmates. _____

If you answered "True" to three or more of these questions, you may be holding yourself back from greater success and happiness due to the unrealistic expectations that you're placing on yourself. In later chapters, we'll present strategies you can use to talk back to your inner critic and begin moving toward the type of opportunities you want.

BECOMING AUTHENTIC

When I was a freshman in high school, a guidance counselor asked me the infamous question, "What do you want to be when you grow up?" I answered that I wanted to be a flight attendant. Without hesitation and with great disdain, she asked me, "Why on earth would you want to do menial work all day like serve food and drinks?" Speechless and ashamed, I didn't have the courage or the opportunity to explain that I wanted to travel to see the world, and becoming a flight attendant seemed like a viable path. In that moment, the expectations of others got in the way of what I wanted for myself. Didn't an adult know better than I did about what was best for me? How could I disappoint my parents and teachers who expected me to go to college and better myself in ways that perhaps they couldn't?

My career choices post-college eventually led me in the right direction toward work that I love in my current field as an executive career coach. But this initial negative reaction about my vocational vision at the time was demoralizing and disorienting. The guidance counselor's rejection of my younger self's career dream had the potential to lead me away from my authentic passions and toward development of a false career persona. A false career persona is formed when you absorb and adopt the expectations of those around you instead of allowing yourself to follow your own intuition about your career options and preferences. The term makes sense when you think about it, since the word "persona" comes from Latin where it means "a theatrical mask." So any time you find yourself donning a "mask," so to speak, by keeping your true career preferences hidden, your false career persona is running the show.

Perhaps you've experienced, like I did, the tendency to shut down potential options, not wanting to disappoint people who you believe have more life experience and wisdom than you do. In such cases, you might be blind to the fact that outsiders' recommendations often have little to do with your unique interests and strengths—they're seeing your life through their own lens of what they consider to be achievement, and perhaps their own missed opportunities as well. In the short-term, cloaking yourself in an inauthentic career persona might not seem like a big deal. Yet if you continue to hide behind a false persona, de-valuing your own dreams about what you want for your career, you may come to realize over time the increasingly heavy personal cost of carrying around someone else's favored career vision.

At the same time, dreams alone are not enough to get you to your career "sweet spot." You might be interested in becoming an astronaut, but if you haven't studied science for the last two decades, your interest in going to outer space is likely not going to be enough to make it happen. What's important here is to seek the alignment between your sense of purpose and your personal strengths, skills, and preferences. Your true career persona straddles the intersection of what you value, what you're good at, and your innate interests. Seeking your *authentic* career persona (and rejecting your false one) is a process that can lead you to the place or places where you ultimately feel good and belong.

For the vast majority of people, your authentic career persona doesn't just show up. The people who know from a young age precisely "what they want to do when they grow up" are few and far between. More commonly, your career persona reveals itself over time. This happens as a natural outcome of working at different jobs and internships, taking classes, and talking to people in various work environments to develop a clear picture of your preferences. Like trying on clothes to determine your personal style and evolving your fashion sense as you move through life stages, your career personality only takes shape after sampling numerous experiences. According to the U.S. Bureau of Labor Statistics,[1] the average worker will have 12 to 15 jobs in his or her lifetime, and that number is projected to grow. Why does this matter? Because it shows that as you grow and change as a person, your work preferences often naturally grow along with you. How authentic is your current career persona? Try the exercise below and find out.

EXERCISE C: YOUR WORK ALIGNMENT QUIZ

Do people tell you how lucky you are to have such a wonderful job, yet you find yourself consistently feeling drained rather than energized by what you do? Does your work feed your spirit as well as your bank account? By examining the statements below, you'll gain a clearer understanding of how congruent your current career is with your inner needs while identifying areas where the fit could be better.

For each question, choose the answer that most closely corresponds to how you feel about your current work. Then read the key below the test to see how closely your job aligns with who you are as a person today.

1. I get excited to go to work in the morning.
    a. Always
    b. Sometimes
    c. Rarely
    d. Never

2. I feel a sense of accomplishment at the end of the day.
    a. Always
    b. Sometimes
    c. Rarely
    d. Never

3. My work is meaningful to me.
    a. Always
    b. Sometimes
    c. Rarely
    d. Never

4. I feel that my work aligns with my values.
    a. Always
    b. Sometimes
    c. Rarely
    d. Never

5. I have the resources to succeed at my job.
    a. Always
    b. Sometimes
    c. Rarely
    d. Never

6. I get so involved in projects that I lose track of time.
   a. Always
   b. Sometimes
   c. Rarely
   d. Never

7. I feel supported and recognized by my manager.
   a. Always
   b. Sometimes
   c. Rarely
   d. Never

8. I enjoy working with my colleagues.
   a. Always
   b. Sometimes
   c. Rarely
   d. Never

9. I feel capable and confident in the work that I do.
   a. Always
   b. Sometimes
   c. Rarely
   d. Never

10. My work allows me to be creative.
    a. Always
    b. Sometimes
    c. Rarely
    d. Never

11. I am optimistic and hopeful about my future career options.
    a. Always
    b. Sometimes
    c. Rarely
    d. Never

If you answered "Rarely" or "Never" to more than five of these questions, the job you're in is likely not the best fit for who you are today, personally and professionally. If that's the case, don't panic. You've probably been feeling like a duck out of water for a long time; the good news is that now you know why. In upcoming chapters, we'll show you ways to identify the career values that are most important to you so that you can better align your work with what gives you the most meaning.

WHAT LEADS TO MAKING POOR CAREER CHOICES

As an example of how your career persona can morph over time, consider the situation of Emily, a client of mine whose career started as an academic. In this capacity, Emily spent the first two decades climbing the traditional ladder of research and publishing. Midway through her career, though, her passion for research started to wane while her growing interest in teaching history and literature caused her to leave the tenure track. Why? Like many people at midlife, Emily realized that she wanted to take on a more direct, empowering, and personally meaningful role. In academia, this meant a shift toward inspiring students through curriculum development and teaching, where she could influence students on the front lines rather than remain a few steps removed from their experience. If Emily had continued along the research track rather than noticing and honoring her new preference for teaching, she would soon have found herself contorting to fit into an outdated—and now false—career persona.

Here are some of the key reasons you might find yourself turning away from your right livelihood and donning a career mask that might stay in place for years:

- **Social yardsticks.** Comparing yourself to others and caving in to their beliefs about career success can lead you to make career choices for the wrong reasons that you'll later regret. The expectations of those around you create what E. Tory Higgins, a professor of psychology at Columbia University, described as the "ought self."[2] In his self-discrepancy theory, Higgins defined the relation between our actual, ideal, and ought selves, the latter of which is based on our understanding of what we think others want us to be. With this in mind, listening to outside opinions over your own inner voice can lead to a misalignment between your desires and those of others, which can lead to feelings of disappointment or even depression. In a misguided attempt to avoid these negative feelings, you might find yourself doing what's necessary to meet external expectations, thus setting off in the reverse direction from where you really want to go professionally.

- **Conflicting messages.** Another way that others may influence your career choices and lead you astray is through conflicting messages. Young people may be particularly influenced by mixed messages received from teachers, parents, and other adults providing guidance, as well as from influential friends and peers. Some people they trust may advise: "Go to the best school," "Get the best job," and "Prioritize a high salary." Others may urge them to "Find your passion," "Dream big," and "Follow your heart." Even if you're a career veteran, you may find yourself trying to sort out confusing messages like these—especially by midlife, a time when you're often encouraged to prioritize finding passion and meaning in your work, yet simultaneously may have more financial responsibilities and family pressures. The resulting lack of clarity can lead smart people to make foolish choices that lead them away from what they really need and want.

- **Imposter syndrome.** Many people—particularly women—go through life with the uneasy sense that everyone else has their career and life figured out except them. If this sounds like you, you might feel like you're fooling everyone who thinks you have professional ability, and that it's only a matter of time until you're revealed as a phony. You might also attribute your success to luck rather than talent or skill, and downplay or discount evidence of your successes. This "imposter syndrome" can even make you step off a track where you're doing well, or lead you to adopt a false career persona in a field you don't like since you feel inadequate in an area that you care about.

- **The creativity conundrum.** Have you ever stopped yourself from starting a business or recommending a new strategy for your team because you believed your idea was not original enough? You might be hesitating to act because you're assuming that unless you can find that one brilliant breakthrough creative idea to make your entire career perfect, then there's no point trying at all. If that sounds like you, then you might be buying into the false cultural message that says some people are naturally more creative than others. The belief that the level of creativity that sparks innovation is inherited or genetic has been around for centuries. The ancient Greeks told stories of the Muses, god-like creatures who reportedly inspired the work of artists, musicians, thinkers, writers, scientists, and mathematicians. Religious writings in many faiths describe creative ideas as being divinely inspired. The vestiges of these ancient beliefs live on today, stopping many potentially creative people in their tracks for fear of not living up to such high standards. Believing such myths can lead you to feel that your work is not good enough, and may deter you from pursuing a career path that you're passionate about.

- **Unrealistic time expectations.** Have you bought into the mantra, "I have to accomplish [X] by age [Y]"? You may give up on your career dreams and set off in the wrong direction if you feel dissatisfied when it takes longer than you imagined to achieve your vision. Perhaps you grew up with self-imposed or social pressure to hit certain professional milestones—such as getting promoted, making partner, becoming a VP, launching a startup, or writing a book—by age 25, 30, 35, and so forth. These unrealistic expectations about how long it takes to succeed professionally may be particularly pernicious for younger professionals, who can feel extreme pressure to reach societally validated goals early in their career—or even make it onto elite lists like *Forbes* "30 Under 30"—to avoid feeling like a failure.

- **Lack of information.** It's easy to jump into a career path without the information you need to make a good decision about fit, particularly when you're just starting out or when you're shifting gears to a new industry. You might think you know what a job will be like when you get there, but if your assumptions are based on too little or incorrect information, you can find yourself climbing the wrong ladder. Let's take my client Marissa as an example. Marissa went into classical archeology, even going so far as to get a Master's degree in her chosen field from Oxford University. But in the end, she decided not to pursue a career in archeology after all because she felt that she needed to get a PhD to do what she originally wanted—and more importantly, she found digging and unearthing artifacts to be much more tedious and boring than she had expected. What had interested her in archeology in the first place? She loved the glamour of Indiana Jones movies and had imagined that she would feel like a female Harrison Ford character if she became an archeologist. But her actual experience on an archeological dig was just the opposite, a perfect example of lack of information leading to a poor fit.

- **Things change.** Your goals at 22 are not the same as your goals at 32, 42, or beyond. Marriage, children, illness, and interests cause people's priorities to shift throughout their career and lifespan. This is to be expected and can even be a good thing—as long as you're willing to shift your career direction as needed to respond to these larger changes. Failing to acknowledge your morphing priorities at different ages and stages can result in goal conflict and career dissatisfaction. Let's take Brenda as an example of how going with the flow of change can keep you from stagnating. When Brenda came to me for career coaching, she had progressed rapidly in her position as an executive in an insurance company. Although insurance was not her passion, she found success in her ability to develop new products. But in her most recent role as chief of staff to the CEO, Brenda found her enthusiasm waning. To her disappointment, the insurance industry was experiencing a time of transition, and the customer emphasis she highly valued was diminishing as a priority for her management team. After evaluating her financial needs, Brenda realized that staying with the company would mean compromising her values. So, she decided to leave and start her own consulting practice. She now feels that she is living true to her values instead of living up to someone else's expectations. Brenda's choice to revamp her career persona in response to new circumstances did not come without its tradeoffs. She gave up an excellent compensation package and benefits at the insurance firm to go out on her own. But she had reached a stage in her career development where the financial security was not worth the discomfort of working toward goals she no longer believed in.

- **Fear factor.** Many people stick with a job that they have outgrown for fear of making the wrong career choice, particularly when it comes to shifting to a new position or industry. This trepidation about change may cause you to stick with the "devil you know" rather than risking a change. Older workers may find it particularly difficult to let go of a career path that

19

they've invested years or decades in even if it no longer brings them joy. Yet a 2015 study published by the American Institute for Economic Research found that 82 percent of those over age 45 who tried a new career made a successful transition. [3] While career change can certainly be scary and comes with a new set of challenges, it's worth remembering that to live your best life and have a career you're passionate about, you need to stretch your capabilities and rise above your fears.

- **Mistaking perfection for excellence.** If you need things to be perfect, they may never get done at all—or even started. A tendency toward perfectionism can keep you from entering the field you want to work in, or from making a needed shift in your career direction. That's because to perfectionists, it's not enough to do something well. Instead of striving for excellence by doing the best that they can do at that time, perfectionists set themselves up for failure because there is always more they could do or could have done. The danger of favoring a perfectionistic approach is that you miss out on the chance to do something well that you enjoy. Instead, you may end up stagnant in your career, stymied by the unattainable goal of perfection.

If in reading this list you realize that your current career choices don't reflect your authentic self, there's no need to panic. A derail can be temporary as long as you notice it and course-correct; it doesn't have to throw you off long-term. It takes trial and error to discover a career persona that fits. It's also common to be unsure what you want early in your career. Trying out different work experiences—even those that may not be to your liking—helps inform your next step. The problem comes when you think you know what you want, but your desires are based on false assumptions. As you'll see in the next section, that's why it helps to develop flexibility in how you think about your options.

GROWING BEYOND FIXED THINKING

Another way that perfectionism can sabotage your career authenticity is through what psychologist, Carol Dweck calls a "fixed mindset"—believing your talents are innate gifts—rather than a "growth mindset"—believing you can develop your talents through your own efforts. [4] If you grew up in a hard-driving family of achievers or with overly demanding and critical parents, you may believe that either you have what it takes to succeed or you don't. Despite how long ago you first heard these messages, you may now hear them echoing in your head and assume that your talents and intelligence are set in stone, for better or for worse.

With this belief system as a backdrop, it follows that if you fail at something—regardless of the multitude of reasons that likely contributed to the failure (some of which may have been beyond your control)—you will interpret the disappointing results to mean that you are not smart. If you are convinced that your capacities are inborn, then you will see errors and mistakes as catastrophic and become convinced that they prove your inadequacy. What's more, your beliefs about your lack of ability may become self-fulfilling prophecies if you then avoid the types of risks that can lead to success, such as taking on roles with greater responsibility or visibility.

This type of inflexible mindset is evident in many high school and college students who tell themselves that if, for example, they don't get into Harvard—or if they don't land a position with the Boston Consulting Group or with an investment bank and make $100K a year in their first job—then their entire career will be a failure. Rather than recognizing that there are many ways to define and achieve career success, rigid thinkers believe their options to be much more limited than they really are.

Ironically, achieving challenging goals generally doesn't ease the pressure for those with a fixed mindset, but instead exacerbates it by upping the ante. As a professor at Stanford University, Dweck describes a condition of perfectionism that she sees among students on campus as "duck syndrome."[5] While these successful students may appear to be moving along smoothly and effortlessly like the top-down view of a duck gliding across the water, the reality is seen beneath the surface: frantic efforts and mad paddling to keep from sinking. Like those with a fixed mindset, those with duck syndrome frequently fail to get the help they need, preferring to keep their perceived shortcomings secret.

To illustrate the severe impact of a fixed mindset combined with unrealistic expectations, a recent survey sponsored by the American College Counseling Association found that 94 percent of responding counseling center directors reported an increase in the number of students with anxiety disorders, clinical depression, and other serious psychological problems. [6] Although the reasons for these increases in mental health issues are complex, college counselors attribute the rise to factors that can be linked to a fixed mindset: unrealistic expectations students set for themselves and their inability to cope with failure, compounded and amplified by social media postings regaling the happiness and success of classmates. Contrary to this counterproductive way of thinking, when you have a more growth-oriented approach, you can put more of your focus into learning and achievement versus worrying what others are doing.

EXERCISE D: WHAT'S YOUR MINDSET?

If you tried the Perfectionism Assessment and Work Alignment Quiz above, these exercises revealed how automatic your behaviors have become. Your thoughts and actions when repeated can become habitual, which allows you to multitask without thinking about it. While efficient, this system can cause problems if you don't stop and question what you are doing and why.

The exercise below will help you evaluate how you generally respond to work situations. Do you tend toward an inflexible mindset that may hold you back in your career, or are you more open to a thinking style that favors growth, which will help you flourish? To find out, read each statement below, and then indicate whether you agree or disagree with it. If you aren't sure, select "Maybe."

1. Your intelligence level is something you can't change very much.
   a. Agree
   b. Maybe
   c. Disagree

2. Your talent is something you can't do much about.
   a. Agree
   b. Maybe
   c. Disagree

3. You can always substantially change how much talent you have.
   a. Agree
   b. Maybe
   c. Disagree

4. People who are good at a particular skill were born with a higher level of natural ability.
   a. Agree
   b. Maybe
   c. Disagree

5. People who are talented in a particular area have spent a lot of time practicing it, regardless of natural ability.
   a. Agree
   b. Maybe
   c. Disagree

6. Intelligence can increase or decrease depending on whether or not you spend time exercising your mind.
   a. Agree
   b. Maybe
   c. Disagree

7. I hesitate to take on new projects at work unless I feel certain that I'll succeed.
   a. Agree
   b. Maybe
   c. Disagree

8. I find taking on new challenges at work exciting because of the possibility of learning new things.
   a. Agree
   b. Maybe
   c. Disagree

9. When I've suffered a setback at work, I am likely to spend more time worrying what others will think of me than taking action.
   a. Agree
   b. Maybe
   c. Disagree

10. When things at work haven't gone as well as I had hoped, I tend to focus on what I've learned from the experience that will help me the next time.
     a. Agree
     b. Maybe
     c. Disagree

11. When I'm not sure how to do something at work, I'm more likely to try and figure it out myself than ask someone for help.
     a. Agree
     b. Maybe
     c. Disagree

12. I am comfortable letting my colleagues and/or manager know when I don't know the answer to something.
     a. Agree
     b. Maybe
     c. Disagree

13. When I give feedback to co-workers, I'm more likely to focus on the outcome of their work than on the strategies they used to reach their outcome.
     a. Agree
     b. Maybe
     c. Disagree

14. When I give feedback to co-workers, I'm more likely to focus on the strategies they used to reach their outcome than on the outcome of their work.
     a. Agree
     b. Maybe
     c. Disagree

If you agreed with questions 1, 2, 4, 7, 9, 11 and 13 (or most of them), then you favor a style of fixed thinking that may stifle your creativity and career potential. If you agreed with questions 3, 5, 6, 8, 10, 12 and 14 (or most of them), then you're more willing to learn from your mistakes instead of catastrophizing when circumstances don't go as planned. If you gravitated toward answering many of the questions with "Maybe," then you fall somewhere in the middle, with room to move further in the direction of growth.

GROWING STRONGER

Having a happy career isn't about having a perfect career. While every job and industry has negative aspects, the key is to avoid seeing challenges as insurmountable problems, or falling back during rough times on a fixed view of yourself as flawed and incapable. My client Martin is a good example of someone who drew on a more flexible mindset to overcome obstacles. Having grown up in a family of doctors, Martin had aspired to become a physician for as long as he could remember. As an undergraduate, Martin's mother died suddenly, and when he returned to school, his mind was not focused on academics. Still, he studied the best that he could for the MCATs and applied to medical school, but he didn't get in. Undeterred, Martin vowed to try again. This time, he was accepted into a PhD program in microbiology. In the third year of the program, he took the MCATs again and reapplied to medical school, but once again was not accepted.

With failure staring him in the face, Martin was confronted with a choice about not only what to do next, but more importantly, how to view his disappointment. One of his advisors explained that medical schools use mathematical algorithms to weed out applicants. Any candidate with an undergraduate GPA below a certain level was automatically eliminated. Because he was not able to stay focused on his work as an undergraduate after losing his mother, Martin's GPA fell below the standard that was required for medical school. Then Martin's advisor asked him a life-changing question: "What would you tell your best friend to do if he was in your situation?"

Martin stopped and thought for a minute. "I'd tell him to move on," he replied. "It's not due to his lack of intelligence that he was not accepted. It's due to circumstances beyond his control." "How can you apply that logic to yourself?" his advisor asked. "I have a lot of options beyond medical school," Martin suddenly realized. "I think it's time I started exploring them instead of blaming myself for not being smart enough."

CHANGING HOW YOU THINK ABOUT SUCCESS

How you think can also affect the work you end up doing. It seems like everywhere you look these days, someone is extolling the benefits of positive thinking. Yet despite this frequent admonition to look on the bright side, some confusion has crept in about the difference between thinking positively and taking positive action. Can merely thinking positively help you land your dream job and make you more successful? Research by Martin Seligman[7] and others has proven that optimistic people do generally enjoy certain benefits over pessimists, from feeling better to performing better at work. But if misused, positive thinking can prevent you from moving forward with your goals, doing more harm than good.

In American culture, you are often encouraged to dream big, pursue your passion, and reach for the stars. Yet while fantasizing about the future does feel good, studies have shown that people who remain living in their fantasies and don't move toward taking action to make them a reality have more difficulty achieving their vision. In fact, research in the *Journal of Experimental Social Psychology*[8] found that people who tried to depict an ideally positive future actually had lower energy than those who didn't mentally imagine this utopian vision. The reason? The former group tricked themselves into believing that they had already accomplished their goal, even when they hadn't in reality, so they didn't feel energized to move forward.

Take my coaching client Gregory, who had always had a passion for photography. Self-taught in his craft, Gregory traveled the world taking portraits of people he randomly encountered, enjoying the relationships that developed as much as the images he captured. His love of photography ultimately resulted in award-winning photographs that were showcased in *Smithsonian* magazine and at the World Bank. Whenever he posted his pictures on Facebook, he'd quickly receive hundreds of admiring comments. Despite this success as a novice, Gregory dreamed of becoming a professional photographer, perhaps securing a plum assignment with a national publication or top agency. Yet a decade later, he was still in the same government job he detested.

Because of his belief in his vision of the recognition and fame that he was sure would come his way without effort, Gregory never took the time to outline the specific steps that would have helped him begin to realize his dream on a larger scale. Imagining that he would suddenly reach the top of the photography world without laying the necessary groundwork, he set himself up for failure because he wouldn't consider less lofty goals that might have brought him satisfaction and success. It was only after he started considering alternatives to the top level and setting goals for achieving them that Gregory was able to move forward as a career photographer rather than a hobbyist.

If you have unrealistic expectations about the power of your thoughts, believing that you can magically make good things happen in your career or ward off disaster simply by thinking positively enough, then you're in for disappointment. While an optimistic mindset can help you achieve your authentic career goals, it's important to be realistic about the actions you must take to move in the direction you want to go. When it comes to finding or creating the career that they want, self-doubters may find themselves falling back on fantasy rather than risking making a mistake. A more effective path toward your dreams involves planning ahead for likely challenges and resolving to stay optimistic when you hit the inevitable bumps in the road.

FINDING YOUR WAY

Wherever you are on your career path today, it is no accident that you've arrived at this juncture. Many factors have potentially combined to influence your journey, including a tough inner critic, social pressures and comparisons, the stage of your career, and fear of change. Yet these influences are only part of the puzzle that will help you find your way to a future of more satisfying work. As you'll learn in the next chapter, the myths you buy into about what makes you happy and what doesn't can also play a major role in the development of unhealthy self-critical tendencies. By understanding and seeing through these myths, you'll be able to move forward toward more genuine career choices that will allow you to thrive at your highest level.

TWO

Career Myths and Confabulations: What Happiness Isn't—and Is

Listening too closely to your inner critic can breed perfectionistic tendencies, which can decrease your happiness quotient at work and in other areas of your life. But other factors also contributed to your current level of career satisfaction (or lack of it). Buying into myths about what supposedly leads to workplace happiness and success can ironically keep you from reaching these very goals.

Take my client Marcia, who started her career at a job she loved as a physician's assistant in a fertility clinic. Helping patients through the trials and tribulations of trying to have a child held deep meaning for her. When she had children of her own, Marcia put her career on hold to stay home and raise them. Twelve years later, she decided to return to work. But what she hadn't anticipated was how much the field had changed during the years she had been out of the workforce. To her disappointment, she found the focus had evolved to put more emphasis on cost and less on patients.

Despite Marcia's dawning realization that the job might not be the best fit for her values anymore, she clung to her fantasy about the field, ignoring its evolution over the past decade. Turning a blind eye to any misgivings that she felt, Marcia applied for numerous positions and accepted a job that seemed promising based on the myth of what she remembered about her former career. But although she was not the type of person to leave anything without considerable thought, within a three-year period, she had quit her job, taken another, and then quit that one too. In explaining to me what went wrong, Marcia unleashed a litany of perceived problems with both situations, including not enough support and supervision from the doctors, pressure to see too many patients, and hours of take-home paperwork.

Undoubtedly, the changes that Marcia witnessed made the situation challenging for those in her industry to continue to do their jobs well. Yet thousands of professionals remained committed to helping patients navigate the new reality. Marcia's belief in the myth about her previous "perfect career" led to her unwillingness to accept that some conditions had shifted. This prevented her from remembering why she had entered the field in the first place: to help patients. Ultimately, Marcia stopped working in the healthcare industry, unable to adjust to the new reality that had replaced the myth in her memory.

To get to the bottom of this type of myth-making, let's look at some research that can help separate fact from fiction by revealing what really doesn't make people happy, and what does. Let's start with the glass half empty.

IT'S NOT WHAT YOU THINK IT IS

With the recent explosion of media attention on the pursuit of happiness, finding ways to feel as good as possible seems to be on practically everyone's mind, particularly in relation to their careers. Yet this has resulted in some unintended consequences. The definition of happiness has become oversimplified, leading many people to expect to find it effortlessly.

So what is happiness really about? When it comes to defining happiness and figuring out how to get it, there are many misconceptions. With career, for example, a common belief is that when you get the next promotion, make more money so that you can buy a bigger house, or receive an industry reward, you'll automatically and permanently be happier. But does achieving such superficial external goals really increase your joy?

Research by Sonja Lyubmirsky[1] and others has shown that focusing solely on a future goal, in fact, does *not* result in greater happiness, and wealth, status, or other external conditions alone don't provide any guarantee of a good life. Despite these facts, our allegiance to myths persist about what we're certain will make us happy.

EXERCISE A: WHAT WILL MAKE YOU HAPPY?

You may think you know the exact recipe for happiness—but do you? Complete the following exercise to see how closely your answers match what social scientists who study happiness and well-being for a living have discovered.

1. You are either born happy or you can't be happy.
   a. Agree
   b. Disagree
   c. Not sure

2. The goal in becoming happier is to feel more positive emotions as frequently as possible and avoid negative ones.
    a. Agree
    b. Disagree
    c. Not sure

3. The more money I make, the happier I'll be over the long-term.
    a. Agree
    b. Disagree
    c. Not sure

4. Happiness comes primarily from attaining significant goals—for example, at work, receiving a promotion or a raise.
    a. Agree
    b. Disagree
    c. Not sure

5. Happier people express gratitude more often than they seek pleasurable experiences.
    a. Agree
    b. Disagree
    c. Not sure

6. People who exercise are happier than those who don't.
    a. Agree
    b. Disagree
    c. Not sure

7. Prioritizing relationships that matter most to me contributes to happiness and well-being.
    a. Agree
    b. Disagree
    c. Not sure

8. Learning and trying new things leads to greater happiness.
    a. Agree
    b. Disagree
    c. Not sure

9. Deliberately setting and working toward personally challenging goals is a significant factor in being happy.
    a. Agree
    b. Disagree
    c. Not sure

10. Happiness and well-being result from pursuing goals that are personally meaningful.
    a. Agree
    b. Disagree
    c. Not sure

If you agreed with all the questions except for the first three, you have a good understanding of what factors are likely to increase your happiness and help you thrive. If you're not sure about many of them, you may need more time to determine what you think you need to be happy and whether it's realistic.

MYTH BUSTING

As a career coach to clients in diverse industries, I've seen firsthand that while people often believe that reaching certain professional goals will make them happy forevermore, this is rarely the case. Among the work-related situations that we expect to create instant and eternal happiness are finding the "right" job and earning a large salary. Yet as research has proven, these myths just aren't true. While achieving such dreams may indeed bring us some sense of happiness (particularly in the short-term), the achievements generally do not result in an ongoing, intense state of joy and well-being.

Take the situation of another client of mine, Selena, who held a position as a senior-level marketing manager in the technology industry. Her goal was to become a vice president of product marketing, having been a director in a respected company for the last four years. When Selena finally reached her goal of becoming a VP, though, she found herself surprised to be feeling miserable. As she reviewed her situation, though, it made more sense—she realized that everyone in the company worked remotely, making her feel isolated and that her manager's expectations were unclear. What's more, the company had experienced frequent reorganizations, which led to Selena having two new bosses in 18 months.

The clues behind why Selena felt unhappy could be found in what was missing from her new position as much as in what was there. But the bottom line was, after the initial excitement of reaching her goal had passed, simply receiving the long-awaited promotion did not lead to the permanently ecstatic feeling that Selena had expected. Instead, other variables related to her workplace, colleagues, and manager still factored in, ultimately leaving her disappointed rather than elated about her new position.

If achievements aren't a sure ticket to better moods, what about cold hard cash? According to psychologist and happiness researcher Ed Diener, higher income improves our mental evaluation of life—which he coined our "subjective well-being"—but not our emotional well-being.[2] Diener found that when it comes to money, once you've reached a certain threshold (up to about $75,000 a year based on research from Princeton University),[3] having more does little to boost happiness. This finding makes logical sense when you think about it—if money equaled happiness, why wouldn't we all just quit our jobs once we reached a financial level of security?

Another myth is that stress is a necessary corollary to success and happiness. You may think you need to prove to others that you're constantly busy and in demand to feel successful. In this 24/7 wired world, you may also feel pressure to respond to emails day and night, sacrificing what little personal time you have so as not to miss out on something you think might be more important. In fact, fear of missing out, or "FOMO," has even earned its own entry on Wikipedia! All of this pressure to be always connected and engaged at a high level is exhausting and stressful. If you look at the data, long-term stress harms our physical health and cognitive abilities like attention and memory, as well as our productivity and creativity. This is certainly not the path to greater happiness at work.

GETTING USED TO A GOOD THING

Let's revisit Selena's situation. Why wasn't she happy once she reached VP level? The answer lies in what psychologists call hedonic adaptation. Simply put, it means that once you reach a goal, although you may feel happier initially, you will quickly adapt to your new reality and return to feeling how you felt before you reached the goal—your baseline level of happiness. To understand this better, think of how you might feel when first setting foot in your brand-new car that you've wanted to own for months. At first, you'd probably feel elated. But the principle of hedonic adaptation suggests that within a week or two of your purchase, you wouldn't feel much different than you did before you acquired the wheels of your dreams.

This was true in Selena's case as well. Once she got used to the fact that she was a VP, the novelty wore off and the problems inherent in any job rose to the fore. Despite her fancy new title, Selena became disengaged from her work and colleagues because she worked remotely and did not have enough opportunity to develop meaningful relationships. She also had little chance to find meaning in her work because her goals were unclear and frequently changing. Earning the title of Vice President was the fantasy about what she thought would make her happy, but the unpleasant realities of her new position quickly overshadowed her initial mood lift.

Selena's experience is not unusual. Many people truly believe that happiness will come once they've finally reached what they imagine is the right level of prosperity and career success. But hedonic adaptation can quickly steal the thunder of these long-awaited dreams. To see if you've experienced the effects of hedonic adaptation in your own career, take the quiz below.

TRY THIS

How many times have you been ecstatic about a significant career move or work situation, then found yourself soon after feeling indifferent or even disappointed in that same scenario? Think back to a time when you experienced a major victory at work, such as landing the job of your dreams or receiving a promotion you worked for years to attain. Then ask yourself the following questions:

1.   How did I feel when I found out that I had finally reached my career goal?

2.   Was I as ecstatic as I expected I would be?

3.   How long did it take before I noticed feeling the same as or similar to how I felt before achieving my long-sought-after goal?

4.   Did I expect the positive emotion to last longer than it did?

If you noticed that you rapidly adapted to your new status and that your joy did not linger as long you had hoped, then you experienced hedonic adaptation.

SO WHAT IS IT?

Now that we have some clues about what *doesn't* lead to happiness, let's turn our attention to understanding what might bring it about. Since ancient times, people have searched for keys to the good life. But modern researchers recognized that to understand the causes and effects of happiness, they first needed to define it to measure it.

While you may think that you don't need a definition of happiness—you'll know it when you see it or feel it—this emotion isn't quite that straightforward. You can get an idea about the true complexity of happiness through a simple Internet search on the word, which yields more than 40 million results. Contrary to popular belief, happiness is not about feeling positive emotions like joy and excitement all the time and avoiding negative ones. It's not possible to authentically feel warm and fuzzy consistently, and even if it were achievable, it would not necessarily be beneficial.

Social scientists can use tools called the Positive and Negative Affect Schedule[4] and the Satisfaction With Life Scale[5] to evaluate the well-being of others. These tools are designed to help people more accurately evaluate their level of happiness, measuring fleeting positive emotions as well as a deeper sense of meaning and purpose in life.

Another way that researchers have helped us understand the roots of happiness is through the PERMA model designed by Dr. Martin Seligman[6], which created the framework for many positive psychology research projects around the world. Since the late 1990s, psychologists have been searching for factors that lead to happiness and well-being. In short, Seligman's research discovered that life satisfaction depends on five key components: positive emotions, engagement, relationships, meaning, and achievement.

Research from Albert Bandura[7] and others suggests that believing that what you do is personally meaningful leads to higher levels of self-efficacy and self-worth. Feeling ownership over your choices, goals, and how to achieve them also leads to greater levels of happiness and satisfaction. In other words, happiness comes from enjoying the journey more than reaching the ultimate goal, whatever that goal might be. Continuously striving for more and more or higher and higher robs you of the ability to pay attention to what you are doing at the moment. When you focus only on the next goal instead of noticing the good things around you and your accomplishments along the way, you're setting yourself up for burnout.

People who set challenging yet achievable goals for themselves report higher levels of fulfillment as they work toward achieving and reaching them, according to a study conducted in Germany by researchers Bettina S. Wiese and Alexandra M. Freund.[8] Their study revealed that people who found their goal hard to achieve reported greater levels of happiness—as well as sense of greater job satisfaction and career success—over a period of three years. With this in mind, it's still important to remember that there's a difference between setting challenging goals and having unrealistic expectations about what you can achieve given the specific variables of a situation.

EXERCISE B: HOW DO YOU DEFINE HAPPINESS?

The way that you think about happiness—and whether your definition of this feeling is based on buying into society's ideas about what makes people happy—can affect your experience of it. Answer the questions below, and then check the key at the bottom to see if your beliefs about what leads to true happiness and well-being are guiding your thought process.

1. I am grateful for what I have on a daily basis.
   a. Agree
   b. Disagree
   c. Not sure

2. To a great extent, I believe happiness is a choice.
   a. Agree
   b. Disagree
   c. Not sure

3. I always look for the good in others.
   a. Agree
   b. Disagree
   c. Not sure

4. I believe things will work out when I try something new.
   a. Agree
   b. Disagree
   c. Not sure

5. I make time for laughter and fun.
   a. Agree
   b. Disagree
   c. Not sure

6. I find it easy to let go of disappointments.
   a. Agree
   b. Disagree
   c. Not sure

7. It's important to rely on others help when I need it.
    a. Agree
    b. Disagree
    c. Not sure

8. I feel supported by the people around me.
    a. Agree
    b. Disagree
    c. Not sure

9. I think that setting goals is key to happiness.
    a. Agree
    b. Disagree
    c. Not sure

10. I believe that my strengths can be developed through hard work and dedication.
    a. Agree
    b. Disagree
    c. Not sure

11. Expressing gratitude is key to my happiness.
    a. Agree
    b. Disagree
    c. Not sure

12. I know what interests and inspires me.
    a. Agree
    b. Disagree
    c. Not sure

13. I am confident in my ability to create the outcome I want from most situations.
    a. Agree
    b. Disagree
    c. Not sure

14. I forgive people easily.
    a. Agree
    b. Disagree
    c. Not sure

If you agreed with most of the statements, then you have a good understanding of the factors that contribute to happiness and well-being. If you're not sure about many of them, then you may need more time to determine how you've been defining happiness and whether it's realistic. If you disagreed with the majority of the statements, read on. Help is on the way!

OTHER HAPPINESS FACTORS

One example of someone who learned how to temper her tendency toward burnout in favor of setting challenging but achievable goals was my client Tracy. A rockstar in the biotech world, when Tracy came to me for career coaching, I noticed that she had an impressive ability to tame the operational chaos in startup environments and rapidly growing organizations. So it was no surprise to me that she wound up leading the complex integration of two companies. After working around the clock for months, the merger was finally complete, and Tracy had time to take stock—more time than she had expected since the acquisition ironically resulted in her position being eliminated.

Upon reflection, Tracy realized that the glamour of such a high-profile position was no longer worth the personal sacrifices she was making, which included a two-hour daily commute. Yet once former colleagues learned that she was "available," her phone continued ringing with new possible opportunities. To her credit, having learned her lesson about the need for balance and self-care, Tracy assessed what was most important to her at that moment in time. Instead of jumping right back into another pressure-cooker job, she courageously decided to start a consulting practice so that she would have more control over her schedule.

The work wasn't easy—Tracy had never run a business and was unsure initially how to move forward. But she recognized that the challenges she set for herself would be achievable with commitment and dedication. When coaching Tracy, I served as her thinking partner to help her set realistic goals and hold her accountable to them. Within three months, Tracy had landed her first client. From her new vantage point, she felt that exchanging a high salary for more control and less chaos in her daily life was a sacrifice well worth making.

Meaningful work and the right level of challenge are important factors in career happiness, but there are other considerations as well, including how competent, autonomous, and connected to others your work makes you feel. A 2015 study published by law professor Lawrence Krieger and psychologist Kennon Sheldon in the *George Washington Law Review*[9] examined the well-being and life satisfaction of 6,200 lawyers. The researchers found that external factors emphasized during law school such as class rank, law review membership, money, or partnership in a law firm showed little to no correlation with career and life satisfaction. Their study also showed that attorneys in large firms and other prestigious positions were not as happy as public service attorneys, despite the former's higher pay and prestige. Highly paid lawyers in prestigious firms also reported more alcohol use.

The public service lawyers described a significantly higher day-to-day mood originating from their sense of service, and greater enjoyment of and perceived meaning in their work. Lawyers in public service also experienced equal life satisfaction to affluent lawyers in prestigious positions. Why did lawyers in public service roles experience greater well-being than the more "elite," highly paid "prestige" lawyers despite substantially lower earnings? We can surmise that more prestigious jobs don't necessarily provide factors noted above as happiness boosters like engagement and meaning

WHY IT MATTERS

As a career coach, I've found that some people question whether striving for a happier work experience is a particularly worthwhile goal. Why should we focus on happiness when there are so many pressing, more "serious" issues to manage in your job and career? But assuming a 40-hour workweek, most of us will spend 30 percent of our lifetime— not to mention commuting, after-hour emails, and vacation not taken—at work. Add to that the reality that almost 70 percent of employees feel disengaged at work.[10] With these distressing statistics in mind, it's easy to see why so many people legitimately care about finding greater workplace satisfaction.

My client Dylan is someone who experienced firsthand the pull toward wanting to feel better at work. With two siblings, Dylan was the only one of the trio without an advanced degree, but he nevertheless out-earned them by 50 percent despite their PhDs and Master's degrees. After reaching VP level in a major financial services company, however, Dylan found himself feeling bored and unenthusiastic about his job, which is why he engaged a career coach.

After taking a step back to inventory his skills, interests, and values, I suggested Dylan craft his ideal job description to capture his current priorities. (See Chapter 6 for more details on how you can do this too.) In doing so, he came to the realization that the following points were most important to him in a job:

1. An organizational commitment to diversity and inclusion.

2. A collaborative team-based approach to problem solving instead of a hierarchical one.

3. The ability to put his strengths of adaptability, risk-taking, and encouragement to greater use.

4. A task emphasis on information security, a topic of personal interest.

Knowing what he wanted from his career, Dylan strategically began to search out opportunities that matched his values. With no urgency to leave his current job, Dylan could take his time to seek out the right opportunity, eventually landing a position that reengaged his interest. His greater feelings of happiness and well-being contributed to his improved productivity. His higher level of engagement helped others in his organization as well as clients that the organization served, and led Dylan to feel reinvigorated in other aspects of his life as well.

You may not always have the flexibility that Dylan had to change jobs. But the important point is that even if you have to stay in your current role, understanding what you value, what motivates you, and what gives your work meaning can help you embrace new and more satisfying tasks. Known as "job crafting," the deliberate reshaping of the job you have into one you want has been shown to enhance job satisfaction and creativity, and even improve health.[11] (We'll discuss more about job crafting strategies in Chapter 6.)

Another client, Mariel, provides an example of someone who found a way to use job crafting to find greater satisfaction at work without leaving her position. In her role as a researcher, Mariel's official job involved developing drugs into commercially marketed treatments. Though she found this work generally satisfying, Mariel had a real passion for mentoring others—yet her research job didn't provide any opportunities for mentorship.

When she heard that her company was searching for someone to head its internal women's leadership organization, she jumped at the chance to infuse new life into the group. Although not part of her official job description, Mariel seized the opportunity to take on this volunteer role alongside her research job. This subtle form of job crafting gave Mariel a way to bring more meaning to her work and greater happiness to her life.

The situations of Dylan and Mariel are not isolated cases, and for good reason. Social science research has proven that the search for happiness is not a frivolous pursuit; on the contrary, positive emotion can create major impacts that reverberate throughout your life far beyond the office. Happiness has a wide range of significant benefits that serve individuals and companies alike, including better health, greater creativity, and improved productivity—and if you don't believe it, studies have proven it.

A review of more than 200 studies found a connection between positive psychological attributes such as happiness, optimism, and life satisfaction and a lowered risk of cardiovascular disease.[12] Research by Ed Diener and Micaela Y. Chan[13] revealed that positive emotion also contributes to a longer lifespan, while multiple studies[14] from the United States and Europe have showed that optimism can result in improved health. Excited to learn more? Some key points about happiness include the following:

- Not only can happiness be measured,[15] but you can play a significant role in affecting your own level of happiness.

- Emotions, both positive and negative, are fleeting. What makes you happy at the moment (or what you think will make you happy) will be short-lived unless it is attached to things that are personally meaningful, involve relationships with others, and are worth striving for.[16]

- Money is nice to have, but doesn't generally increase your long-term happiness beyond your need to cover the basics.[17]

- The more that you strive for goals that are intrinsically motivated, the more willing you'll be to act on them to derive a sense of accomplishment and purpose.[18]

As you begin to recognize various career fallacies under which you may have been operating, think about how these false mental constructs may be holding you back from feeling your best during your workdays. In the next chapter, we'll expand our exploration of how you got here by examining the role of expectations you may hold about your career, and how to keep these hidden biases from sabotaging your career goals.

THREE

How Your Hidden Biases Can Hurt Your Career

Man is disturbed not by things,
but by the views he takes of them.

—Epictetus (AD 55–AD 135)

You've now seen how self-criticism—often without your awareness—can cause you to set your sights on unrealistic career goals that make it nearly impossible to win against your internal critic. You also now have much clearer insight into the myths and expectations that can keep you from true happiness at work, as well as which characteristics and choices are associated with greater satisfaction and well-being. Let's next examine how failing to recognize and address your own hidden biases can lead to missteps when it comes to making authentic career choices, and how to get better at authentic decision-making.

WHO'S MAKING YOUR DECISIONS?

A year out of undergraduate school, my client Marie entered the workforce with the energy and enthusiasm of an idealistic 23-year-old. Despite the tight job market, she was offered a coveted rotational training program by a high-profile Boston financial services company. Before accepting the position, Marie did question whether it was too analytical for her background—the job required an expert at number crunching and data analysis. Marie knew that math was not her strongest suit, but she put her doubts about her fit for the role on the back burner. After all, the company recruiter assured her that she could succeed in the role without a math or computer science degree, and a chorus of friends and family chanted, "This is such a great opportunity!" "You are so lucky to have gotten into this company!" So swayed was she by the opinions and excitement of others that Marie said yes and took the position against her better judgment. Just seven months later, feeling burned out and confused, Marie made the difficult decision to leave her job cold turkey, acknowledging after the fact what a poor fit it was for her.

What happened to Marie is not uncommon. You may recognize her dilemma, having made past decisions based primarily on what other people thought you should do. It's easy to miss the hidden biases in others' opinions and fail to weigh those accurately against what you know objectively about your own strengths and passions. If you've ever taken a job that you didn't really want because you didn't trust yourself enough to find a position that was the right fit, then you understand this from personal experience. Perfectionism—which pushes you to try to look good to others and make decisions based on external appearances rather than values alignment—can be the enemy of good decisions.

Why is it so easy to fall into this trap? It's common to make choices based on a wide range of factors that you may not even be aware of, from peer pressure to a desire for approval. These tendencies make it difficult to make solid decisions based on what's really right for you. Most people seek some measure of certainty in life, but perfectionists in general have more difficulty making decisions for fear that their choice will be the wrong one. As a result, they may stay in limbo too long and miss out on opportunities. On the flip side, some perfectionists may push away feelings of doubt and uncertainty, jumping into decisions simply because doing something—even the wrong thing—feels more comfortable and less threatening than not having answers. Neither is a great strategy for career planning; a better approach lies somewhere in the middle. With that in mind, try the following exercise to see what's influencing your decision-making today.

EXERCISE A: HOW DO YOU MAKE DECISIONS?

In order to see how hidden biases may be hurting your career and whether you are overly influenced by outside opinions, it is important that you begin to understand how and why you make the choices you do. Do you tend to narrow your focus without realizing it, or base your decisions on a set of inaccurate assumptions? Do you involve others or prefer to go it alone? The questions below will help you uncover biases that may be hindering your ability to make optimal career choices:

1. After I make a decision, it's final, because I trust my intuition is strong.
    a. Agree
    b. Disagree
    c. Not sure

2. To succeed in business today, it's essential to make decisions as quickly as possible.
    a. Agree
    b. Disagree
    c. Not sure

3. I tend to have a strong "gut instinct," and I rely on it when making decisions.
    a. Agree
    b. Disagree
    c. Not sure

4. I'm sometimes surprised by the outcome of my decisions.
    a. Agree
    b. Disagree
    c. Not sure

5. I generally make important decisions at the last minute.
    a. Agree
    b. Disagree
    c. Not sure

6. When making a decision, I consider various options in terms of my goal.
    a. Agree
    b. Disagree
    c. Not sure

7. I rarely make important decisions without involving other people.
    a. Agree
    b. Disagree
    c. Not sure

8. I assess a variety of possible solutions before I make my decision.
    a. Agree
    b. Disagree
    c. Not sure

9. I make decisions in a systematic and logical way.
   a. Agree
   b. Disagree
   c. Not sure

10. If I have doubts about my decision, I go back and recheck my assumptions and my process.
    a. Agree
    b. Disagree
    c. Not sure

If you agreed with questions 1 through 5, you might be relying too much on what you think of as your "gut instinct" and not enough on facts and the perspective of others. Read on to learn strategies to make more objective decisions and release yourself from thinking you have to know it all. If you agreed with questions 6 through 10, you understand the value of widening your options, considering what can go wrong and the importance of having a plan. Bravo! You'll learn more about how to maximize these positive tendencies in this chapter. If you're not sure about many of these answers, you may need more time to sharpen your decision-making skills. The rest of this chapter will help guide you.

WHAT'S KEEPING YOU FROM LISTENING TO REALITY?

In certain fields, a high percentage of people decide to leave a chosen career—some soon after starting—despite a high investment in education, time, and resources. It's clear that something is amiss with our ability to make career decisions that will stick. Take teachers, for example. Several studies have estimated that 40 to 50 percent of new teachers leave within the first five years of entering the profession, and that more than 9 percent leave before the end of the first year.[1] And remember the lawyers we discussed in Chapter 2? Twenty-four percent of JDs who passed the bar in 2000 were no longer practicing law in

2012, according to an American Bar Association study of almost 5,000 lawyers.[2] These trends suggest that there's a lot of room for improvement in our decision-making skills when it comes to our careers.

Besides peer pressure and a predilection for wanting the admiration of others, there are additional factors that may be keeping you from making realistic career choices that may cause you, like Marie, to ask "How did I get here?" just a few months after starting what may have seemed like a dream job:

- **Low-hanging fruit.** Taking Marie's case as an example, think about how seeing only what was right in front of her—rather than considering the many other options she might have explored—kept her from dreaming bigger. In Marie's case, looking only at the opportunity that was presented during her senior year of college at the insurance company, limited her potential. Since she believed that it was best to have a job by graduation, she didn't investigate other options that might have been a better fit. With the insurance company position as the low-hanging fruit, she was blinded to the possibility of additional better choices.

- **Assumptions.** When confronted with a big decision, many people have a natural tendency to quickly call on a set of assumptions about the situation and then seek out information that confirms and reinforces their beliefs. In cognitive science, this inclination is called "confirmation bias." Getting back to Marie, in retrospect she had remembered initially questioning the appropriateness of the insurance company position as a match for her talents and interests—so much so that she had asked the recruiter before accepting the position whether someone without a substantial math background could succeed in the role. When the recruiter confidently told her that she could be successful, her confirmation bias was validated. Marie's friends and family also triggered her confirmation bias by echoing their belief that Marie was being offered a special opportunity, tipping the scale enough for Marie to accept the position.

- **Emotional reactions.** When you have a tough decision to make about your job, you may find your head spinning with conflicted feelings as you replay the same arguments for and against the decision over and over in your head. At times like this when your feelings are churning a mile a minute, it's easy to be emotionally swayed, which can lead you to make the wrong career move like Marie did. She liked the idea of working for a reputable company and getting started in her first position, as well as the validation she received from her family, friends, and recruiter. Because she got sucked into these feelings (which passed quickly once the reality of the poor fit became clear), she made a decision that was a poor fit with her skills and strengths.

- **Guessing games.** When you lack knowledge about the big picture, it's tempting to make guesses about the future based only on what's in your current frame of reference, leading you to draw poor conclusions. It's easy to hear only what you want to hear and ignore everything else. And if we look once more at Marie's situation, we can see that guessing about her limited math abilities—egged on by her recruiter—led her to take a job for which she wasn't strongly qualified. While she initially recognized her limitations in data and quantitative analysis, Marie downplayed the importance of these quantitative skills to convince herself that she had enough ability to succeed in the role—a guess which in retrospect she realized was unwise.

HOW CAN YOU MAKE BETTER DECISIONS?

As you can see, it's not easy to make authentic career choices with so many outside forces clamoring for your attention. How can you cut through the noise of these external influences to avoid getting derailed from a career path that's right for you? Again, let's turn to Marie's situation to visualize ways you might overcome your natural biases when faced with a significant career decision:

- **Expand your views.** To combat an overly narrow focus, it makes sense to work on expanding your viewpoint by becoming aware of more options. To do so, it can help to find someone who knows your field and can help you think about additional choices you wouldn't normally consider. Ask yourself what you would do if the possibilities you are currently considering didn't exist. In Marie's case, what other options might she have pursued if the insurance company job wasn't an option? She might have continued applying for other positions, followed through with a few other interviews that she had landed, or continued researching the types of careers that would fit well with her educational background and skill set. Within the widening context, ask yourself what you really want. Practice listening to your intuition—if you sense red flags in an opportunity like Marie did regarding her math skills, don't ignore them. Instead, think about what options could be a better fit for who you are.

- **Test-drive your hunches.** Making untested predictions and basing decisions on guesses rather than data can lead to poor career choices. What if Marie had talked to someone doing the job she was offered before she accepted? What if she had the opportunity to see what the job really required, especially in terms of math skills? How might that have affected her decision? Another way to reality-test is to ask questions that may disprove your assumptions. In Marie's case, she might have asked, "On a daily basis, what types of number crunching and data analysis will I be expected to do?" Taking steps like these that give you actual answers to your questions can lead you away from crystal-ball decision-making.

- **Separate yourself from the emotions.** How you feel in the moment can be misleading as a barometer for long-term choices. Marie, imagining herself working for a prestigious Boston company and taking home a sizable paycheck, temporarily tricked herself into forgetting her concerns about the skill set required. One way out of this dilemma is to gain distance on the issue by shifting perspectives away from your personal conundrum. Instead of focusing on the pros and cons of your own decision, ask yourself, "What would I suggest that my colleague do?" By remaining too close to the issue and emotionally embroiled in it, you may turn a blind eye to your intuition's early warning system. The fact is that your assumptions may be wrong if you're basing them on your current feelings.

- **Feel out the future.** Another strategy for not becoming a slave to your emotions is to consider how you'll feel about the decision down the road. Can you picture yourself a year into the job? Imagining your feelings in the future provides distance between today's emotional intensity and the possibility that you might feel differently tomorrow. Once you've created a buffer from those feelings, you can develop a wider perspective on the decision rather than basing it on narrow assumptions or how you feel today.

TRY THIS

Think back to one of your career decisions that didn't work out the way you thought it would—perhaps a job you accepted or one you left.

Candidly write down your answers to the following questions to explore why the choice you made didn't go as well as expected.

1. The career choice I made was to:

   _____

2. The options I considered before making the decision were:
   a. _____
   b. _____
   c. _____

3. My top 3 values I thought about in contemplating this decision were:
   a. _____
   b. _____
   c. _____

4. The people I consulted with about my career direction were:
   a. _____
   b. _____
   c. _____

5. The contingency plan I developed was:

   _____
   _____
   _____
   _____

6. The incorrect assumptions I might have made were:

   _____
   _____
   _____
   _____

7.   I may have been overconfident about:

_____

_____

_____

_____

Do your answers provide a clue as to how you might be able to make a decision that works better for you in the future? Obviously, you don't get a redo when it comes to your current job and past career decisions, but knowing how hidden biases or emotion may have clouded your previous judgment can serve you better in the future.

IS THERE A MODEL FOR A HAPPY CAREER?

Making career decisions based on biases and assumptions can lead to regrets. But aside from learning to override these factors, how can you give yourself the best chance of choosing options that will lead to career happiness?

Research by James K. Harter et al[3] has shown that finding fulfillment at work leads to feelings of well-being, lower burnout, and greater entrepreneurial creativity. These are wonderful findings, yet I've often seen clients take information like this in the wrong direction—toward an overemphasis on finding the perfect career fit, the pressure of which adds to their anxiety. Still, there is no doubt something to be said for taking time at the outset to identify an opportunity that's congruent with your unique values and preferences. More recent research by Chen et al[4] has looked at exactly how people find fulfillment. For some, it's important to find work that closely aligns with their values and interests before committing to an opportunity. Others are comfortable believing that they may grow to enjoy their work more over time. The most important thing is to understand what *you* find meaning in, and which values, interests, and relationships are most important to you.

One way to think about career satisfaction is by considering what makes up your personal "sweet spot." Think of your sweet spot as the intersection between your interests/passions and your natural skills/strengths, which cannot be separated entirely from what people will pay you to do (market needs). Keeping financial concerns in mind is important to finding viable employment down the line. But without a firm grasp on your own passions and skills—and making those elements account for around two-thirds of your analysis when making career decisions—happiness will likely elude you.

Here are some additional ideas you can use to help with career decision-making as you strive to develop a model for your ideal job. Consider your opportunities in light of these questions to help reduce the possibility of basing your career decisions on the wrong things:

- **How does the opportunity make you feel?** When you need to make a difficult decision relating to your work, consider whether choosing one way or another makes you feel better. If thinking about a specific choice generates a sense of peace, pleasure, and/or satisfaction, those are good signs that you're on the right track toward an authentic career move. If, on the other hand, thinking about a specific outcome of the choice makes you feel negative emotions such as fear, doubt, or resentment, then you have a clear signal of what not to do.

- **How interested and engaged do you feel about the work?** A desired outcome of any career decision you make is to result in a state of engagement where you "lose yourself" to a job or project because you are so absorbed by it. So when faced with career options, think about whether your decision will likely result in an opportunity for this type of absorption in your vocation. If you're choosing a career path solely for external reasons, such as prestige or what others think, this is an indicator that you're on the wrong track with your decision-making.

- **How connected do you feel to potential colleagues?** During the interview stage or other preliminary steps in a career decision, you may feel a disconnect with the people you meet during your meetings, or with the company or industry that you're considering joining. It's important to pay attention to these red flags, as they are indicators that the opportunity may not be a good fit for you. The relationships you have with the people you work with are a critical part of career happiness. As mentioned in Chapter 2, Seligman's PERMA research found that those with meaningful, positive relationships with others are happier than those who do not,[5] and this is as important in a career context as in a personal one.

- **Does the opportunity feel meaningful?** While there is something to be said for simply paying the bills, if it comes down to a choice between a position that fulfills your sense of personal mission or "just a job," the meaningful opportunity is more likely to lead to long-term happiness. When you serve a cause bigger than yourself or find a way to help others through your labor, you're feeding your soul and thus increasing your own chance of happiness.

- **Do you expect to feel challenged?** Is the opportunity that you're considering going to give you a sense of achievement? If so, it will help you feel greater professional and life satisfaction. Think through each option in front of you and determine whether those you're considering are likely to result in striving to better yourself in some way. Choose opportunities that you expect can lead to a sense of personal accomplishment that you feel on the inside, rather than just external accolades for doing something you've already mastered.

GETTING CREATIVE WITH YOUR CAREER

In the early 2000s, researchers Amy Wrzesniewski and Jane E. Dutton conducted a study[6] that looked at how employees could take a more active role in finding meaning and satisfaction at work. They discovered that people who took steps to customize their roles to better fit their interests and strengths found greater meaning and enthusiasm for their work. In other words, employees who crafted their roles by taking creative license with their "one-size-fits-all" job description were more likely to be engaged and flourish long-term in their career.

As we touched on in the last chapter, customizing your role—or job crafting—changes the meaning of what you do by changing job tasks or relationships in ways that enable you to reframe the purpose of your job and thus to experience work differently. My client Diane's situation offers a good example of effective job crafting. Diane is an audit manager who oversees a group of 30 certified public accountants for a global engineering company. Diane views her role as a defender of the employees in her organization. She views the audit function as one that can prevent fraud, protecting the company's intellectual capital and the people who work for it. Over time, Diane extended her role by reaching out to the community to speak to students about careers in accounting, as she was passionate about inspiring the next generation.

Diane used the questions above to help craft her position that resulted in her greater job satisfaction:

- By focusing on the value she brought to her company, employees, and the next generation of accountants, Diane experienced pleasure and enjoyment.

- By seeing her role as protecting her company and its employees—and by sharing her knowledge and passion for the profession with the community-at-large—Diane experienced greater absorption and meaning in her job.

- By widening her involvement in professional and community organizations, Diane built new positive relationships.

TRY THIS: DISRUPT YOURSELF

Do you understand how to make a decision so that it 1) aligns with what you really want, 2) adds to your capabilities and experience in a beneficial way, and 3) creates new opportunities for you and others that will be exciting and helpful? Use the following question set as a framework to help you disrupt your habitual patterns of decision-making and tap into your intuition.

When faced with a big decision in your job or career, ask yourself:

- Does my decision give me a sense of peace, pleasure, and/or satisfaction?

- Will this choice fuel feelings of connection to my work?

- If I go in this direction, will I be able to build positive, meaningful relationships with colleagues?

- Does this option provide me with the opportunity to serve a cause bigger than myself or fulfill my sense of personal mission?

- Will this decision give me a chance to be challenged and experience accomplishment?

If you answered yes to more than half of these questions, you're on the right path toward making a decision that will more likely result in a happy outcome.

BEYOND YOUR BIASES

It's not easy to make authentic career choices, especially in light of how many outside forces are vying to move you in a different direction. But with practice, you'll get better at learning to recognize when you're being influenced by bias or short-term emotions, and you'll more naturally take steps to widen your focus and avoid overconfidence when you don't have enough information about an opportunity. And by getting good at asking yourself the right questions, you'll have a framework for disrupting your usual decision-making style before going in the wrong direction.

You're now ready for real change! In Part II of the book, you'll learn some advanced strategies for rumbling with your inner critic, starting with the next chapter that focuses on recognizing and defeating common thought patterns that may be keeping you stuck after suffering a career setback.

FOUR

Got "Mental Gremlins"? Overcoming Negative Self-Talk

As a successful sales manager and one of the youngest women to have risen rapidly in a fast-growing technology company, I was given responsibility for managing the relationship with a major New York City–based bank—you'd recognize its name. I was 28, and the average age of most of my clients was 50. The bank's Chief Information Officer was no fan of my company, having worked for our principal competitor for over 20 years. One Sunday morning the phone rang—it was our national Vice President of Sales. "Can you explain the article on the front page of today's *Boston Globe*?" he asked. I had no idea what he was referring to. "The article where *your* customer says we have the worst salespeople in the industry?" "Oh my God," I thought. "This is the end of my career. I'm a failure."

I can still recall the pit in my stomach and the shame that washed over me that day. Many things contributed to my client's CIO publicly humiliating my company and me, but all I could see was what *I* did wrong, which led to my mistaken belief that I would never recover from this particular failure. This type of career-related shame, though damaging to our personal and professional self-esteem, is not uncommon—perhaps you too have your own "mental gremlins" that have been holding you back based on a perceived career failure. In her book Rising Strong: *The Reckoning. The Rumble. The Revolution*, shame researcher and author Brené Brown cites research in which 85 percent of the men and women interviewed could recall a school incident from their childhood that was so shaming that it changed how they thought of themselves as learners.[1] In particular, half of the respondents could point to a specific incident where they were told or shown that they weren't creative.

When colleagues or clients don't value your contribution at work or try to shame you based on a mistake or shortcoming, it's easy to internalize their message. But it's important to remember that your inherent worthiness as a person and professional isn't based on the judgment of others. Keep that important point in mind as you read through this chapter, which explores several factors that can keep you from being your best and most authentic self at work. We'll also provide ideas on how to recognize and overcome these obstacles so that your perceptions of the past don't keep you from your ideal future. To get started, try the exercise below, which will help you begin to identify thought patterns that may have morphed into mental gremlins.

EXERCISE A: IDENTIFYING YOUR MENTAL GREMLINS

Has an unexpected experience at work left you ruminating about whether disaster is around the corner? Do you wake up at night worrying that you might lose your job? Answer the following questions to find out if unhealthy thinking patterns like these are causing needless worry about your career, or if your fears may be well-founded:

1. My manager's attitude toward failure can best be described as:
   a. It's an important part of learning.
   b. Mistakes are OK to a certain degree, but not many of them.
   c. Fail and you're a goner.

2. Do you feel appreciated by your manager?
   a. Yes, my boss praises my accomplishments on a regular basis.
   b. I could use a few more pats on the back.
   c. My hard work goes unnoticed.

3. Does your manager trust your work?
   a. Yes, my boss asks me to take on important projects and provides opportunities for visibility.
   b. My boss occasionally asks for my input.
   c. No, I'm ignored most of the time.

4. If you feel like you're about to get fired, your evidence includes:
   a. I don't have any concrete evidence; it's just a feeling I have.
   b. There's a new management team that wants to take the company in a new direction.
   c. I'm no longer asked to attend important meetings.

5. After you make a mistake at work, your manager:
   a. Sets up a one-on-one to talk with you about what happened and how to prevent it in the future.
   b. Publicly berates you in front of your peers.
   c. Stops copying you on emails and avoids conversation.

6. Do you have accomplishments that are noticed by your boss and team?
   a. Yes, in the last year, many of my ideas to improve business processes or outcomes have been recognized and implemented.
   b. A few of my ideas have been used.
   c. My opinion is rarely considered.

7. Is your department vital to the organization?
   a. Yes, very much so.
   b. My group is important but not critical.
   c. No, there have been rumors of downsizing in my department.

8. Is your company/organization financially healthy?
   a. Yes, we are a leader in our industry.
   b. We've had a difficult year, but things are turning around.
   c. Our organization is facing a lot of financial problems.

9. How was your most recent performance review?
   a. Excellent—and I also received a substantial raise.
   b. Average—I met expectations.
   c. Not so hot—I'm on a performance improvement plan.

10. Your relationship with your co-workers is:
    a. Excellent—we collaborate on most everything.
    b. Good—I get along with everyone but prefer not to socialize.
    c. Poor—there are conflicts, so I keep to myself and avoid interaction.

If you answered "a" to most of the questions, there's little evidence that you're job is at risk—so if you feel jittery anyway, it's a sign that your mental gremlins are very active (and convincing). It's time to learn strategies to push back on them. If you answered "b" to most questions, you're likely not in immediate danger, but don't rest on your laurels—you have work to do to earn more trust and recognition. If you answered "c" to the majority of questions, your gremlins might be right. It's time to put a plan in place to improve your situation or move on.

UNDERSTANDING CAREER SHAME

While failure is expected when you dare to take risks in your career, it's important to differentiate between the disappointment you may temporarily feel after a specific setback, and a feeling of shame that you may internalize and carry forward with you as baggage throughout your professional life. The *Oxford Dictionary* defines disappointment as "the feeling of sadness or displeasure caused by the non-fulfilment of one's hopes or expectations."[2] When defined in this way, disappointments generally refer to an external source—a person, event, or thing—that has triggered this feeling. But shame is more of an inside job.

Research in **neuroscience** and **moral psychology** suggests that feeling shame is the result of your unconscious, emotional, morally judging brain system—"interpreter" modules in the left hemisphere of your brain—telling you a baseless story about your worthlessness that you believe. This means as much as you may want to manage your feelings of shame, it can be difficult between the size of your unconscious emotional and moral intuition and your own ability to convince yourself that you've indeed done something wrong.

To put this science into context, think about what happens when you start a new job or business. If you're like many people, you begin the launch phase entertaining a fantasy that all of the hard work you've expended will automatically result in your dream come true. Rarely do things happen this easily and smoothly. Veteran entrepreneurs will tell you that succeeding requires continual testing of and adjusting to the market. In fact, research shows the failure rate of executives coming into new companies to be as high as 30 to 40 percent after 18 months.[3] If you're going to outlast those odds, you need to stick with it and be prepared to weather market downturns. You can expect to feel disappointment from time to time, but there are things you can do to avoid riding the shame train, such as understanding how you perceive "failure."

EXERCISE B: LEARNING FROM FAILURE

Think back to a time when you suffered a setback at work—perhaps on a project that was late or had negative results, a situation where a client was dissatisfied and threatened to go with the competition, or a time when you wanted a promotion or job that you didn't get. Regardless of the setback, answering the following questions can help you gain insight into how you perceive your failures and how quickly you bounce back from them:

1. Describe the setback you experienced:

   _____

   _____

2. How did you feel immediately after the setback?
   a. Very disappointed and sad.
   b. Disheartened.
   c. Humiliated.

3. What was the first thing you did after realizing your mistake?
   a. I told my boss and offered a plan for how to correct the situation.
   b. I told my boss.
   c. I kept it as quiet as possible.

4. What actions did you take after the failure?
   a. I solicited feedback from trusted colleagues on what I might have done differently.
   b. I'm still licking my wounds.
   c. I'm focused on finding out who threw me under the bus.

5. How did you feel 30 days after the failure?
   a. Disappointed but accepting.
   b. Still sad, but better than a month ago.
   c. Humiliated.

6. What did you learn from this setback?
   a. I'm resilient and can grow from this experience.
   b. I have more to learn.
   c. I'm a failure and will never be able to live up to my boss's expectations.

7. What plans do you have to recover from this setback?
   a. Evaluate if I'm in the right position and if I need additional training.
   b. Develop a plan for preventing a similar situation.
   c. Hope that it blows over quickly.

Your answers to these questions will provide insight into your perspective on career setbacks. If you answered "a" to most questions, you understand that setbacks, although unpleasant, are an important part of growing and learning. This growth mindset will enable you to bounce back from the inevitable twists and turns that are part of every productive career. If you answered "b" to most questions, you might find it helpful to get away from the issue, even for a short time, by doing something enjoyable—perhaps taking a walk, listening to music, or exercising to put it in perspective. You'll come back to the problem with a fresh point of view. If you answered "c" to most questions, you might be suffering from a perfectionistic view of the world, not truly buying into the reality that setbacks are part of success. Read on to learn strategies for separating disappointment from shame.

DISMOUNTING THE SHAME TRAIN

Failure feels terrible, as do the sadness and anger that may accompany a setback. While it's important to acknowledge these feelings and grieve what might have been, you don't want to get stuck in the wallowing stage. In my personal example above, I lived with career shame for far too long but eventually recognized the value of transitioning to a more forward-thinking mindset. I reorganized my sales team to better serve the needs of my CIO client and eventually developed a positive relationship with her. But my change in perspective didn't happen overnight; it was necessary to do some hard work first in order to move out of the shame-blame cycle. If you get stuck in a similar pattern, here are a few strategies to help you change how you're thinking about a perceived failure:

- **Focus on what you can learn.** Failure can make you feel so discouraged that you lose perspective. If you shift to figuring out what you can learn from the experience and determine how it will help you grow, you can short-circuit the shame-blame thought process. Recalling the fixed versus growth mindset that we discussed in the first chapter, expecting yourself to never fail is a sign of fixed thinking. It occurs when you internalize the belief that you either have what you need to succeed already or you never will followed by the shame that results from your negative assessment of your own skills and abilities. A healthier approach is growth-oriented thinking, where you focus instead on what you've learned from the setback that can help you eventually develop your talents and advance your career.

- **Avoid all-or-nothing thinking.** When you are focused on getting the ideal role, you risk falling into an all-or-nothing trap. You may talk about "finding" the perfect job, but secretly you hope it finds you. This type of thinking may lead to stagnancy, instead of staying open to different possibilities and continuing to explore options.

- **Don't "should" on your career.** To keep yourself off of the shame train, you might also consider whether you're expecting to find perfection in your career choice if you don't have this same assumption in other aspects of your life. Think about whether your standards are higher for your professional life than for your personal life, and try to lessen your sense of what you "should" be doing.

- **Figure out what you want.** Many of my clients talk about wanting to find the perfect fit for their career, yet when I ask them to describe their ideal job, they have no idea what it would look like. When you don't know what you're looking for, it's very hard to find it. This is one reason that the pursuit of "career bliss" can leave you feeling inadequate and disappointed. To avoid this problem, spend time figuring out what you're really looking for before you set off to find it.

- **Don't buy into the bumper sticker.** "Follow your passion." "Choose a job you love and you'll never work a day in your life." These clichés are good for magnets and bumper stickers but not necessarily for your career. These simplistic statements suggest that finding the right fit is easy, and recognizing your job bliss happens like a bolt of lightning—one minute you're confused, and the next minute you know exactly who you were meant to be. The fact is that passion-worthy jobs are built over time, not instantly found. It makes sense that you might feel shame about failing to find your perfect career when faced with societal

73

pressures that assure you it can—and should—be easily and quickly done.

FOSTERING PASSION

Striving for a good career fit is a more realistic goal than striving for a perfect one. Finding the right fit is often an unpredictable trial and error process, but paying attention to your passions—both professional and personal—can help lead you in the right direction.

So if you agree to spend time fostering your passion instead of expecting to magically find it, how do you go about it? Here are some ideas to get you started:

- **Shake up the world.** If you feel confused about the right livelihood, instead of asking, "What do I want my next career step to be?" ask instead, "What problems do I want to help solve?" or "How do I want the world to be different?" These questions shift the focus from a self-involved perspective to one that looks at the wider world, with purposeful work in mind. People are wired to find relevance, significance, and value in their lives. In a study on intrinsic motivation, participants who expressed both high interest in their job along with concern for others averaged more than 50 percent more hours of overtime than those who didn't.[5] Understanding the greater impact of your work—and why you decided to pursue and put time into that work—will help you enjoy the tasks and become more satisfied. Remember Emily from Chapter 1, the academic who left the tenure track? As interested as she may have once been in researching early American history and literature, she found greater meaning in communicating her knowledge to students rather than publishing in academic journals. At a crossroads between climbing the academic ladder and getting off the tenure track to stay true to her purpose, she chose the latter.

- **Make the most of it.** If you look for it, every job offers the opportunity to gain knowledge, learn new skills, and inform your interests and values. Even when you find yourself in an environment that's not a great fit for you, staying focused and trying to maximize your experience can help you ultimately transition toward work that feels meaningful to you. Your reputation will follow you wherever you go, so it's a smart choice to stay positive and make the best of your current situation. Remember that when Emily decided to pursue teaching instead of research, she did so because she loved teaching and interacting with students. At the same time, she didn't drop the ball on her research job; she waited for the right opportunity to transition gracefully into a role that was more personally meaningful.

- **Know what you like.** In their book *The Power of Interest for Motivation and Engagement,* scholars K Ann Renninger and Suzanne Hidi explain that for the most part, interests are developed, not uncovered.[4] Scientists have learned that passions and interests take time and experience to blossom fully. Many now famous people didn't find their groove until well into their thirties and beyond. The message here is that if you feel you're not in the right vocation yet, it's not unusual. It's also not impossible to make changes, no matter your age. But you first need to find a way to identify your authentic interests, and then take action toward moving your career in a direction that honors those preferences. The following exercise can help you explore what those interests might be, if you aren't sure yet—we'll also get into much more detail about examining your interests and values in Chapter 6.

TRY THIS

Retroactively mapping out your career path to date might help you identify latent interests that can guide you toward job joy. To get you started on this exercise, I'll share my personal career path, which has been as unpredictable and circuitous as any you can imagine.

Graduating with a BA and Master's in music, I knew the likelihood of making it as a performing artist was small, so I took a teaching job. After two years of teaching, I realized that it was not for me. I knew that I needed and wanted to make more money and couldn't afford to go back to school. After an enormous amount of networking, I was hired by Xerox into their sales development program. Although I changed employers, I stayed in technology sales and marketing for the next 15 years, which I hated most of the time.

When the company I worked for was acquired, I was laid off. I knew what I didn't want to do (technology sales), but not what I wanted to do. So I leveraged my business development background and was hired by a university to open a business for their executive education program, and then recruited to another university to develop relationships with employers for their business school.

During this last role, I started informally coaching students. Most of the conversations were about the students' hopes and aspirations, focusing on how they could reach their goals and remain true to themselves. Finally, the light bulb went on. Coaching others to be their best selves at work was what I loved and wanted to do! The piece that only became clear over time was that *building relationships* was at the core of what I enjoyed and valued. It took a wide variety of trial-and-error experiences to reveal my core interests and develop a true conviction about them.

Now it's your turn. Write about the jobs you've held so far, noting any feelings that you have about what you've done or are currently doing (hating it, loving it, feeling indifferent, etc.) Are there specific roles—or even a single aspect of a job or industry—that hint at clues about what you really enjoy—or alternatively, what you want to move away from?

EMBRACING UNCERTAINTY

The philosopher Voltaire once said, "Doubt is an uncomfortable condition, but certainty is a ridiculous one." When people seek career advice that they hope will lead them to the "perfect fit," they are expressing their discomfort with uncertainty. The desire to know what's coming next is hardwired in humans.[6] The human desire for certainty likely has its roots in prehistoric days, when knowing where to find food, shelter, and safety were paramount and often meant the difference between life and death. Our brains have evolved to find it rewarding to discover information that feels "certain." In fact, not knowing something feels stressful, which is why we strive to decrease that uncertainty whenever possible. The problem is that while seeking more information may feel like forward momentum, in reality, when taken too far, it can actually be a way of delaying taking concrete action.

Successful career transitioners develop strategies for limiting uncertainty, but they don't expect to avoid it completely. My client Brett is a good example. As a business development professional, Brett entered the biotech industry with a non-scientific background and secured a position with a service provider to the biopharma industry. After developing one of the most successful networking events for biotech professionals in the Boston area, Brett developed a vast network of professional contacts in the industry. Facing a crossroads in his career, he wanted to determine if he could make a move to a business development role in the industry and see what gaps in his training he'd have to fill in. So Brett strategically tapped his contacts to ask what skills he needed and how to best position himself to become an attractive job candidate in his new area of interest. This informal research gathered from his professional peers helped Brett fill in some gaps, limiting ambiguity and helping him move forward in a more informed way, even though the ultimate outcome remained unclear.

When uncertainty can make decisions difficult, it's easy to globalize not knowing one thing to feeling as if *everything* is up in the air even when it isn't. People who excel at managing uncertainty start by taking stock of what they know and what they don't know, assigning a factor of importance to each. They gather all the facts they can and take their best shot at compiling a list of unknowns, as in Brett's example.

Sometimes career changers want to quit their jobs out of frustration without thinking through the consequences of jumping into the water without a life jacket. They assume, often wrongly, that their next best job is waiting for them and if they simply untether themselves from an unsatisfying situation, they will find it. The reality, though, is that they often feel overwhelmed by the uncertainty they face once they've left the security of their last position.

Taking steps toward incremental change can help you manage the unknowns of major transitions. Career transition programs such as PivotPlanet and Encore.org offer incremental steps to ease career transitions, enabling people to learn the ropes in their new field while transferring skills they developed in the for-profit sector. PivotPlanet introduces would-be career changers and entrepreneurs to people working in their professions of interest to learn from their mistakes and advice. Encore.org offers fellowships for mid-career and later professionals who want to transition to the not-for-profit sector.

EXERCISE A: REDUCING UNCERTAINTY

Although you can't control every variable in your career, you can reduce the uncertainty of those things that you can directly influence. Answer the following questions with "Yes," "No," or "Somewhat" to see if you've considered ways to overcome the risk of moving forward. The more "Yes" answers you have, the better you are at reducing uncertainty.

1.   I'm passionate about my purpose.   _____

2.   I'm clear on how it will benefit others.   _____

3.   I know who my stakeholders are.   _____

4.   I have a plan to get from where I am now to where
     I want to be.   _____

5.   I've identified things that potentially can go wrong
     and have come up with "what if" scenarios for each.   _____

6.   I've identified people who can challenge my
     assumptions.   _____

7.   I'm willing to take a risk to get where I want to go.   _____

RE-STORYING YOUR PAST

Another way of creating a new future is by changing the way you look at the past. My client Ed is a mid-career marketing manager who had a successful track record working for high-tech start-up companies. Without warning, Ed was laid off from his most recent job and was told that his dismissal was not performance-related. Following a perfunctory meeting where he handed over his badge and laptop, he was given 10 minutes to clean out his desk and was then escorted to the door with a box of his belongings in hand. In recalling what happened, Ed said that he felt that he was treated like a criminal. The experience left him shocked and angry. His confidence shaken, he voiced the possibility of leaving the high-tech industry, convinced that he must have done something wrong to have caused his employer to lay him off.

During times of extreme stress such as a job layoff or job-related failure, it's not uncommon for the primitive, self-protective part of your brain to go into overdrive. Whether due to genetics, brain chemistry, your experiences and coping skills, or a combination of these factors, it's easy in such situations to succumb to negative self-talk. You might find yourself ruminating, thinking the same unproductive thoughts over and over. The more prone you are toward self-critical and pessimistic thinking, the more that pattern becomes automatic. Think of a small stream with tributaries feeding it. Over years, that stream can become a river because of the water deepening and widening the river bed. The deeper your pattern of catastrophizing, the more likely it is to be activated by a setback.

When you find yourself thinking negative thoughts repeatedly, recognize it for what it is: a mental pattern that has been established over time but that can be changed. With attention and practice to what psychologists call cognitive reframing, you can establish more positive patterns of self-assessment. Research[7] has shown that this practice of reframing or "re-storying" leads to the development of new neural networks dedicated to positive thoughts, which can decrease anxiety. In fact, people who practice reframing have been shown to have better mental and physical health, as well as a higher level of life satisfaction.

One way to achieve reframing is to write about the situation to help you gain perspective and find your career footing again. This is, in fact, what Ed did. Putting his thoughts in writing about the trauma of leaving his position at the startup enabled Ed to gain perspective on the initial devastation he felt. This practice led him to look in a more balanced way at the factors that led to his departure. Ultimately, despite his disappointment about his last job, Ed chose to stay in the technology field and is still thriving eight years later.

Not convinced about the value of using writing as a strategy to process your emotions related to career failure? Consider the fact that it might also help you land a new job faster. In a study[8] of 100 engineers who had been laid off, researchers used a writing experiment to see which type of approach led to quicker recovery from the setback. One third of the group was instructed to note in a diary how they spent their time each day. The second group was asked to write down their deepest feelings about the loss of their job. The third group was given no writing instructions at all. Among the second group who vented about their anger and disappointment on paper, more than a quarter found a new job after three months. Among the other groups, a much smaller percentage found work, even though all the participants expended the same amount of effort in their job hunt and got the same number of interviews. And more recent research shows that writing about stressful or traumatic events can even have positive long-term effects on your immune system and blood pressure.[9] If you're feeling inspired, give the two writing exercises below a try:

TRY THIS

Instead of dissecting your failures after the fact, try visualizing from the front end that things have been a flop. Imagine that you fail spectacularly at a change you're attempting, such as a career transition or starting a business. Create a list of all the things that you think could go wrong, from no employers responding to your applications to a competitor setting up shop across the street from yours one month after your launch. Next, write down all the steps you would take to mitigate these disasters. Figuring out what could go wrong ahead of time can help you manage the risk of uncertainty and keep you from failing in the first place.

EXERCISE B: WRITING ABOUT FAILURE

Think back to a time when you felt ashamed or deeply disappointed about a failure you experienced. Spend at least 15 minutes a day for five days recalling these emotions and delving into your deepest feelings about the situation. Then answer the four questions below. As you do so, don't worry about grammar, spelling, complete sentences, or repetition. Don't purposely try to find meaning in your perceived failure; if you do, great, but if you don't, don't worry. By writing out your feelings about the incident, research suggests that you are likely to bounce back more quickly than you would if you ruminated about the situation:

1. What happened?

   _____

   _____

2. How did you feel about it?

   _____

   _____

3. Why did you feel that way?

   _____

   _____

4. How might you deal with a similar situation in the future?

   _____

   _____

When it comes to your career, you don't have to fall victim to negative self-talk and fear—a strategic approach can help you move beyond perceptual stumbling blocks about "failure" so that you can find an authentic job fit more quickly. In the next chapter, we'll take a closer look at how tapping into your strengths can help guide you toward happier workweeks. Later in the book, we'll also learn more about how science, in examining how people thrive, offers insight about the best approaches for defeating specific types of mental gremlins.

Part Two

REDEFINE

FIVE

Career Strength Training: Making Your Work Better By Using What You Do Best

Once you're ready to become more true to yourself in your professional life, understanding your personal and professional strengths can help point the way toward greater career happiness. The concept of strengths is one of the most exciting in the field of positive psychology research, and it offers tremendous possibilities for helping you identify the qualities of a career that are most likely to result in fulfillment. Strengths are qualities that you're good at and often come naturally to you. Strengths that you enjoy using will energize you, which can lead to great work.

If you feel you have a specific "life purpose" or career mission, your strengths are likely related to this area. One clue that you are using your strengths is that you feel alive and excited. Using your strengths is associated with a long list of well-researched benefits including greater self-esteem, vitality, and well-being.[1] This chapter will help you identify specific strengths that when applied at work can help you enjoy your job more while generating feelings of autonomy, competence, confidence, and self-esteem by doing what you naturally do best.

USING YOUR STRENGTHS:
THE KEY TO WORK-LIFE SATISFACTION

Have you ever found yourself so engaged in an activity that you lost track of time? Did you notice feeling energized no matter how long you spent on the endeavor? Regardless of whether the deep level of involvement happens when you focus on certain tasks at work (such as writing, presenting to an audience, performing a science experiment, or designing a website)—or when you're involved in a hobby (like gardening, yoga, painting, or singing)—research[2] shows that your feelings of enthusiasm and engrossment are a sure sign that you were tapping into one or more of your strengths.

While it's true that strengths are things you do well, there's more to it than that. You can be good at something yet find it draining or unfulfilling. For example, let's say that your job requires that you write a monthly status report. You find yourself procrastinating each month as the deadline approaches. While writing your report, you feel your energy flagging and you check Facebook repeatedly. Finally done, you review your report. It's a solid job—clear and to the point—and your boss compliments your writing style. Yet the process of getting there felt arduous to you—even though the results of your efforts paid off in quality work, you didn't enjoy creating it. Your negative reaction to report writing is a clue that this type of administrative task may not be a strength that you want to pursue in your career.

The topic of strengths and their benefits at work has been widely studied. Researchers have shown that using your strengths at work leads not only to higher job satisfaction, but also to increased productivity and organizational loyalty.[3] This research also showed a connection between use of strengths and an improved ability to cope with work stress.

ROAD TO A BETTER CAREER MATCH

Here's an example of the role of strengths on the job: my former client Charlotte is an MD trained as an anesthesiologist and pain management specialist. As a clinical physician, Charlotte spent much of her time in the operating room administering anesthesia to patients. By her own admission, Charlotte told me that while she always paid close attention to patient safety, she sometimes felt bored in a role that required close monitoring and little else. Another part of Charlotte's job, however, was training medical residents. Unlike how she felt when administering clinical procedures, Charlotte loved this aspect of her job. She would spend countless extra hours helping students, taking their phone calls and preparing materials for them.

Recognizing that Charlotte was at a career crossroads, her employer engaged me as her coach to help her map out her next career move. In our work together, I recommended she ask 15 people who knew her well to recall a time when they saw her at her best, list the strengths they noticed her using, and send her an email recalling the memorable occurrence. The feedback Charlotte received was remarkably consistent. The majority of people talked about Charlotte's gift of teaching and mentoring, along with her ability to take difficult concepts and explain them in a way that was easy to grasp. Prior to receiving this input, Charlotte was seriously considering looking for another clinical role in anesthesiology. Reflecting on the perspective of others helped her realize that her strengths lay elsewhere, and as a result, she decided to become a career coach with a focus on working with physicians who are unhappy in their jobs. Today we are colleagues in the coaching world!

Let's examine how uncovering Charlotte's strengths enabled her to make a better-informed career decision, for her own benefit as well as those with whom she works. Charlotte knew that she derived more satisfaction from teaching than clinical procedures, but she didn't have a lens through which she could identify and name her strengths. As discussed in Chapter 3, seeing only what's right in front of you and making assumptions are the enemies of good decision-making. Charlotte's request for input from co-workers offered a counterpoint that widened her focus and steered her away from her initial plan to follow the most familiar path, which she ultimately realized would not have been the best one for her.

Organizational scholars have found that when managers understand their employees' strengths and match job tasks to those strengths, the workers are more confident and motivated to perform at their highest level.[4] People who understand their strengths are also better prepared to match those capabilities proactively to the needs of their organization. Remember Diane from Chapter 3, the accountant who expanded her job responsibilities to include speaking in schools to encourage students to enter her field? Diane called on her strengths of vision, mentoring, and encouragement to add interest to her role, and she was able to experience greater meaning and satisfaction in her work as a result.

EXERCISE A: REMEMBERING YOUR STRENGTHS

Think back to a time at work when you felt you were thriving. Perhaps it was a period when you were surrounded by a collaborative team that you were proud to be on, or you achieved an accomplishment that had personal meaning and made you feel gratified. Perhaps you felt so involved in an activity that the hours passed without you noticing. Once you've immersed yourself in the memory of that positive experience, answer the following questions:

1. What was the situation that came to mind, and what made it so memorable?

    _____

    _____

    _____

2. What did you notice about your energy level when you were engaged in this endeavor? What feelings do you recall having at that time?

_____

_____

_____

3. What strengths did you draw on to achieve the outcome? (Some examples of strengths include tenacity, compassion, vision, communication, and organization—or you can also look at a fuller list of strengths later in this chapter to help you identify your top strengths.)

    a. _____

    b. _____

    c. _____

4. What three adjectives would others use to describe you?

    a. _____

    b. _____

    c. _____

5. What percentage of the time are you able to use your strengths in your current job? Check one:

    a. 10%–30%

    b. 30%–50%

    c. 50%–75%

    d. More than 75%

Times when you felt on top of your game, in the zone, or at your best point to signs that you were using one or more of your strengths. Identifying those situations and the strengths that you employed are vital to helping you pinpoint what makes you the most satisfied in your career.

In reviewing your answers to questions 1 and 2, can you recall the feeling of pride and satisfaction you felt when you achieved the goal that was so important to you? Do you recognize the strengths you used to achieve that outcome (question 3) and how others would have described your strengths (question 4)? If it was difficult to answer questions 3 and 4, you may not yet feel confident naming your strengths. Read on for suggestions on how to get clearer. If you answered question 5 with a or b, your current job may not be maximizing the use of your strengths. Chapter 6 will help you identify strategies for reshaping your role to better fit your capabilities.

WHAT IF YOU DON'T KNOW?

Are you reading this and thinking, "I don't know what my strengths are?" Rest assured, you're in good company. When I ask clients to tell me their greatest abilities or reflect on their most significant accomplishments, many admit that they aren't sure, or attribute their success to "just doing the job." When something comes relatively easy to you, you may take it for granted and not notice it as much. So here are a few tips to light your way toward recognizing your own strengths:

- **Watch for signs of excitement.** When you engage in an activity in which you have true talent and interest, your excitement is palpable. One way to identify your strengths is to notice when you feel energized and expansive. The more motivated you feel, the more likely it is that you're drawing on a core strength.

- **Notice when you're more creative.** In a situation where you are using your strengths, a blast of creativity may kick in to allow you to take a unique, novel approach to solving a problem. To recognize your strengths, pay attention to those innovative moments and give a name to your capabilities.

- **Take time to experiment.** Think beyond your job description and consider new tasks that you'd like to take on. Are you a scientist who wants to empower female employees? Then volunteer to run your organization's women's leadership network. Are you a software developer who wants to help clients use technology more effectively? Then offer to work on your company's client consulting team. If you are excited about trying something new and you have some indicators that you'll be good at it, give it a try and see how it goes. You just might discover a strength that you've been under-utilizing.

- **Ask colleagues to give you feedback.** Trusted co-workers or mentors may have a clearer sense than you do of when you appear most animated and enthusiastic. Ask them to let you know when they notice that you have a high level of engagement. Look for common patterns in the feedback you receive from different people to create a portrait of your strengths.

- **Take a strength assessment.** If after trying the steps above you want more personalized guidance toward unearthing your strengths, some well-designed assessment tools can help you out. Two effective and widely used tools are the VIA Character Strengths Survey[5] (you can access a free version of this survey at http://www.viacharacter.org/www/Character-Strengths-Survey) and the Gallup StrengthsFinder,[6] which is a talent assessment based on the bestselling book *StrengthsFinder 2.0* by Tom Rath.

EXERCISE B: YOUR PERSONAL STRENGTHS LIST

Having the right language can also help you hone in on your true talents. Below is a list of common strengths. Use this to help you devise your own personal list of strengths. When writing out your list, don't feel constrained by the words below. Feel free to come up with your own terminology, using this list as a launching pad:

- Confident
- Conscientious
- Strategic
- Responsible
- Action-oriented
- Caring
- Empathetic
- Motivated
- Organized
- Trustworthy
- Bold
- Disciplined
- Fearless
- Artistic
- Visionary
- Focused
- Inspiring
- Analytical
- Patient
- Creative
- Enthusiastic
- Observant
- Entertaining
- Communicative

WHY CARE ABOUT STRENGTHS?

You may feel that since your strengths come naturally to you, they aren't important enough to pay much attention to. Some people prefer to focus on overcoming their perceived weaknesses rather than building on their abilities as a path to success. But consider that individuals who use their strengths every day have been found to be six times more likely to be engaged on the job, according to the Gallup Organization.[7] Other research has shown that more than 70 percent of employees who believe their managers can name their strengths feel engaged and energized by their work.[8]

Gaining awareness of your top abilities and setting goals for how to use them can help you feel more enthusiastic and committed to your work. Unfortunately, Gallup's data also showed that less than 5 percent of respondents set goals based on their strengths or had managers who reinforced and encouraged building on those strengths.[9] Clarifying your strengths and helping your supervisor understand the benefit of leveraging them can have huge payoffs for your career and your company!

TRY THIS

Now that you've listed your top personal strengths above, think about how you'd like to use them. Are there some talents that you'd like to use more, or abilities that you're using too much? To clarify how you'd like to leverage your strengths in the future, answer these five questions:

1. My top five strengths are (revisit your personal strengths list from Exercise B):

   a. _____

   b. _____

   c. _____

   d. _____

   e. _____

2. A project or activity in which I'd like to use one of my top five strengths is

   _____

3. One strength that I'd like to use more of is:

    _____

4. One way in which I can use the above strength is to:

    _____

5. The steps I will take in the next 30 days to better align my strengths and job include:

    a. _____

    b. _____

    c. _____

    d. _____

In the next chapter, we'll explore how your values and the things you find meaningful are also key to finding greater happiness in your career.

SIX

Examining Your Values: Seeking Purpose Every Day

Remember Marcia back in Chapter 2, who started her career in a job she loved yet ultimately ended up leaving the industry? Vast changes in the field caused her to become disillusioned and disappointed when she returned to work after taking time out to raise her family. Marcia's perfectionistic tendencies were part of what led to the problem, but something else was going on here behind the scenes, too.

Marcia's inability to adjust to the new reality of patient care was, at its core, a conflict of values: her values versus those that the industry had evolved to prioritize. Fifteen years prior when she started her career, it was a different world. Healthcare providers were able to spend time getting to know their patients and building enduring relationships with them—in other words, prioritizing patient care, which was an immutable value for Marcia.

Fast forward to today, when new economic realities had made the patient-provider relationship more transactional than caring. The level of distress Marcia felt at this industry-wide sea change that prioritized cost-cutting above all else conflicted sharply with her own patient-centered values and approach to service. The idea that she couldn't spend the time with patients that she thought was necessary to provide optimum care was more than someone like Marcia—who saw her career and life mission as helping others—was willing to accept. That massive disconnect between the industry's evolving values and her own is what led her to decide to leave a field she had once loved.

FINDING MEANING IN WORK

There are as many reasons why people don't like their jobs as there are jobs themselves. Bad bosses top many people's lists of gripes, alongside difficult coworkers, limited resources, employer demands to work increasingly long hours, and ethical challenges that may force employees to choose between corporate profitability and doing the right thing. Despite these objections, work provides an important source of meaning to many people. Within jobs themselves, recent research has shown meaningfulness to be *the most important aspect* of work to employees, trumping pay, rewards, recognition, promotion opportunities, and even working conditions.[1]

As we've learned in earlier chapters, being able to find meaning in your work is a key factor in creating a positive work experience. Instead of pursuing happiness which is actually the result, not the cause, of well-being, a more effective approach is to instead seek meaning, value, and purpose in what you do each day. But if it were that simple, everyone would be doing it. What *is* meaningful work exactly, and how can you find more of it? Research findings[2] on what employees in 10 industries found meaningful may surprise you:

- **Meaning represents a complex range of emotions.** Contrary to conventional wisdom, meaningful experiences are not always pleasant. Seeking relevance through meaning is not about searching for the holy grail of happiness, but searching for depth and connection with others. Though feeling happy may become a byproduct of a positive work experience, such as colleagues recognizing the contribution you made to a project, meaning can also be linked to difficult situations. People who report meaningful personal experiences often talk about challenging or even heartbreaking situations, such as nurses or doctors helping grieving family members after the death of a loved one.

- **Meaning isn't just for CEOs.** The researchers discovered that finding significance in the work you do has nothing to do with your education, position, or level. Hospital workers who deliver meals or empty bedpans can find importance in connecting with patients just like doctors and nurses can, and sanitation workers can find satisfaction in contributing to cleaner and safer neighborhoods.

- **Meaning is personal.** Meaningful experiences aren't the same for everyone—such experiences are intensely personal. What gives one person a sense of purpose could be meaningless to someone else. Often when people talk about finding meaning in their work, they're confusing meaning and mission. Meaning, as you can see from the examples above, can come from almost any type of work. It's great if you also have a mission that you're passionate about—but not everyone has the luxury of working for a purpose-based organization, and expecting every workday to be memorable is unrealistic and unfair.

- **Meaning comes and goes.** Experiencing work as meaningful doesn't always happen on a consistent basis, let alone a daily one—it tends to be much more episodic than that. So just because you have a bad day today, it doesn't mean that you won't have something happen tomorrow that creates a sense of meaning for you. Often that "wow" feeling is connected to making a difference to someone else, persisting in a difficult situation, or solving a complex problem. Although these special experiences may be periodic—or even few and far between—they can have a profound impact on the way you feel about your work. As a coach, when clients thank me for helping them successfully move forward with a difficult career transition or attain a promotion they were working for months to achieve, I often think, "It's amazing that I get to do what I love!" This doesn't mean that I don't have frustrations and disappointments in my job like everyone else—but these peak moments keep me connected to the larger significance of what I do, which helps me put annoyances big and small in perspective.

- **Meaning is best understood in retrospect.** A sense of meaningfulness is rarely experienced as significant at the moment the event takes place. In the research mentioned above, it was only *after* the interviewees were asked to recall a particularly significant work experience that they were able to make the connection between an event and its larger impact on their lives. An experience or achievement may seem inconsequential at the time it happens, but years later could turn out to be highly meaningful to you or others.

EXERCISE A: ARE THE CONDITIONS RIGHT FOR YOU TO FIND MEANING IN YOUR JOB?

Sometimes the culture and management tone of your organization can help you foster meaningful experiences and connections. Other times, your work environment makes it tough to access those opportunities. Let's take a look at the company or organization you currently work for to see which side of the fence you're on. Are you likely to experience moments of feeling that you're in the right job at the right place at the right time, or is your workplace setup more liable to make you wonder, "What's the point?"

Answer the following statements with "True" or "False" to gain insight into the aspects of your work that most often to lead to meaningful experiences, and the likelihood of finding them with your current employer:

1. I understand what my organization contributes.
   a. True
   b. False

2. I understand the values that underpin my employer's business.
   a. True
   b. False

3. My employer walks the walk, not only talks the talk.
   a. True
   b. False

4. I understand how my job fits with the larger purpose of my organization.
   a. True
   b. False

5. My manager helps me understand how my role contributes to the broader whole.
   a. True
   b. False

6. My organization does a good job at keeping tedious tasks (i.e., filling out forms, report writing) to a necessary minimum.
   a. True
   b. False

7. The culture of my company is supportive, respectful, and inclusive.
   a. True
   b. False

8. I am able to give and receive positive feedback, feel a sense of belonging, and appreciate how my work positively impacts others.
   a. True
   b. False

9. The values of my company are in line with my own.
   a. True
   b. False

10. I have the leeway on my job to decide how to go about doing the work.
    a. True
    b. False

If you answered "True" to the majority of these questions, then your organization's culture supports the climate you need to thrive. If most of your answers were "False," then your current work environment may not be supportive of what you need to find meaning and flourish in your job.

CRAFTING YOUR JOB TO FIND MORE MEANING

Imagine that you're a software engineer whose primary responsibility is to write software applications. You've noticed that when you have the opportunity to talk with customers who use your company's product, you have a talent for explaining how the technology can help them without putting them to sleep with technical jargon. When a customer responds appreciatively, you feel that you've made a real difference. This helps you experience a sense of meaning in your work, so you ask your manager for more client-facing opportunities.

Or maybe you're a trained musician who loves to perform. While you do get some opportunities to play music professionally, economic realities don't allow you to pursue your craft full-time. So, in addition to your nighttime gigs, you take a job at a community college teaching courses on pop music and the history of jazz. When you're at the podium presenting to your students, you feel the same high as performing for an audience.

Or picture yourself working for an automobile manufacturer. You like your job but sometimes you ask yourself, "Who knows or cares what I do?" At lunch with a co-worker, she reminds you that ensuring cars are built to proper safety standards helps save lives every day.

These three scenarios are examples of what psychologists call job crafting. As touched on in earlier chapters, job crafting is a deliberate method of redesigning your existing job to play better to your strengths, values, and interests. In other words, it's a way of actively customizing your job by modifying tasks and changing interactions with others.

Job crafting is an excellent strategy if you're in a job that you like but don't love—or if you're in a job that you don't think is an ideal fit but you can't leave right away—because crafting the role to better meet your needs has been shown to increase employee satisfaction and engagement.[3] The primary ways that employees can craft their jobs are by:

- Expanding or limiting the tasks on which they focus

- Changing their primary work relationships or job-related interactions

- Using "cognitive crafting" to think about the value and meaning of the work they do and how it fits into the larger goals of the organization

To get your feet wet with cognitive crafting, try out the exercise below.

TRY THIS

Consider your current job situation. Spend five minutes thinking about what's working versus what you wish were different about your position. With those points in mind, answer these questions:

1. What tasks would you like to minimize?

   _____

   _____

2. What tasks would you like to add?

   _____

   _____

3. What relationships would you like to develop or deepen?

   _____

   _____

4. How might you craft or design your job (or parts of your job) differently to connect your actions and duties more closely to your own personal mission and values—or the mission and values of your organization—in order to derive greater meaning? (*Hint: think of the hospital workers described above who found meaning by linking it to the importance of connecting with patients and their families.*)

   _____

   _____

WHAT DRIVES *YOU?*

Now that you understand the types of strategies and circumstances that can lead to meaningful work experiences, it's time to drill down into identifying your own unique core values that—when prioritized through your job—will help you have an easier time connecting with that meaning. Your core values are beliefs and ideals that are fundamentally important to you as an individual. They can help to shape your identity and ideally will drive your behavior and choices both inside and outside of work.

To help identify your values, it helps to focus on some of their shared characteristics such as:

- **Affecting how you feel.** Your values affect how you feel depending on whether you follow your values or disregard them. For example, if independence is an important value to you, you'll likely feel upset if someone challenges your independence, despairing when you are unable to protect it, and energized when you can exercise this value. When Marcia (who we met in Chapter 2) felt that her ability to help patients—one of her core values—was compromised by her inability to spend more time with them, she felt dismayed and discouraged, leading her to quit the profession.

- **Motivating action.** When you feel strongly about a value, it can inspire you to do something about it. For example, some people who hold social justice and compassion as important values pursue goals to achieve tangible accomplishments in this arena, like working toward civil liberties for all or trying to change legislation related to human rights. If social justice and compassion are values that you care about, then specific actions you might take in your career could be to look for work in a nonprofit devoted to equality and social change, or volunteer for a political party or candidate whose mission you believe in.

- **Varying in importance.** A value for one person is not necessarily a value for someone else. When you think about what is important to you in life, you likely place importance on different things than your colleagues. For some people, achievement, salary, and promotion are paramount, while others may place a higher value on finding ways to achieve security, compassion, or novelty through their vocation.

Operating outside of your personal value system can also cause your level of motivation to drop. It's hard to feel energized about work that doesn't reflect who you really are and what you care about. Even if you receive external rewards in exchange for your efforts, the lift you get from that is likely to be temporary. Ultimately, when your goals don't reflect your true values, it often leads to disillusionment, as in the case of Marcia above.

Research published in the *European Journal of Social Psychology*[4] has shown that successfully living in alignment with your values increases personal well-being. A disconnect between your personal values and those of your employer or work group was shown to be a major cause of a sense of uselessness and meaninglessness at work. Values alignment, on the other hand, can lead to feelings of satisfaction and meaning in your career.

With that in mind, let's spend some time determining *your* core values, which can help you better pinpoint your passions, interests, and areas of meaning. By knowing what you truly care about, you'll be armed with important information to help guide your career choices.

EXERCISE B: IDENTIFYING YOUR CORE VALUES

Read the following list of values, then pick up to five values that are the most important to you and prioritize them. (If your core values aren't mentioned here, you can list others in the spaces provided at the end of this list.) For those you selected, write a few sentences on why these values are significant to you, and describe a specific time in your career when you were aware of their importance. Psychologists have found that people who reflect in writing on their core values have greater motivation to reach their goals.[5] So once you have identified your core values, keep your list close at hand and commit to using self-affirmation to write about your goals and intentions regularly.

- Autonomy
- Determination
- Growth
- Excitement
- Leadership
- Wealth
- Loyalty
- Wisdom
- Pleasure
- Spirituality
- Fairness
- Responsibility
- Steadfastness
- Popularity
- Optimism
- Leadership
- Humor
- Balance

- Adventure
- Beauty
- Friendships
- Kindness
- Empathy
- Service
- Power
- Stability
- Focus
- Knowledge
- Security
- Challenge
- Health
- Recognition
- Achievement
- Status
- Love
- Learning

My top 5 values are:

1.
2.
3.
4.
5.

These values are significant to me for the following reasons:

Value 1:

_____

_____

Value 2:

_____

_____

Value 3:

_____

_____

Value 4:

_____

_____

Value 5:

_____

_____

Describe a specific time in your career when you were aware of the importance of each of these values:

Value 1:

_____

_____

Value 2:

_____

_____

Value 3:

_____

_____

Value 4:

_____

_____

Value 5:

_____

_____

RECIPE FOR HAPPINESS

The work you've done in this chapter to understand what brings you meaning, as well as the importance of values and how to identify your own, can serve you well throughout your career. Staying true to your core values and beliefs while doing your job can lead to a sense of autonomy, control, and competence, all of which can improve your sense of well-being over time. When you work in an environment that shares your values, you'll not only likely benefit from more social support and reinforcement of common views, but you'll also be aligning your actions with what truly matters to you. This facilitates career happiness and can lead to greater success.

Once you've identified your most cherished values, the next step is to be sure that your own thought patterns and actions support them. Certain emotions can keep you from fully owning and exercising your core values at work. In the next chapter, we'll explore how to use your emotions strategically—including the fear and anxiety that often accompany having the courage to manage your career and live your life with passion and purpose.

SEVEN

Three Cheers for Negative Feelings at Work: Using Emotions Strategically

Throughout this book, we have emphasized the benefits of well-being and meaning as a path toward greater work satisfaction—which they certainly are. But as noted previously, all types of emotions are fleeting, and feeling happy all the time is neither realistic nor desirable. In fact, from my experience as a coach, I've noticed a trend with my clients: the more internalized the pressure people put on themselves to see only the positive aspects of their career, the more generally dissatisfied they're likely to be. What's more, negative feelings can provide a valuable source of career intelligence if you listen to them. When you experience emotions like stress, fear, and guilt, they can steer you toward making needed changes in your professional life.

I vividly remember coaching a client named Claire. For weeks at a time, Claire would cry in my office, bemoaning her work situation that made her feel frustrated. She knew that her job in product development and marketing was sucking her dry. The position neither allowed her to use her strengths nor reflected her values. She felt little kinship with the organization's mission, which focused on maximizing profits, while her passion was helping people break through personal barriers and flourish. Claire's uncertainty about what she wanted magnified her dissatisfaction and made it difficult to move forward. As Claire's coach, I wanted to help her find ways to manage her pain but also understood that out of struggle often comes clarity. Over time, Claire's feelings of futility subsided as she became more certain, step by step, about what actions she could take to shape her future direction.

Without experiencing confusion, self-doubt, and anger, Claire might have become too comfortable—or at least complacent enough to stay in a position that was deeply unsatisfying to her. Though her extreme dissatisfaction with her career reality was very difficult to experience at the time, it was what gave her the push she needed to alter her direction and ultimately reach a better place. As unpleasant as her raw feelings were, they provided Claire with invaluable information about her job situation. She was then able to leverage those insights in deciding to pursue other opportunities that were a much better fit for her strengths and values.

Claire moved through and beyond the muck of confusion in two ways. The first was by not dismissing or avoiding her unpleasant feelings. The second was by spending time figuring out where to go next—setting goals to help her uncover alternatives that were both viable and desirable to her. Since she was at a puzzling crossroads, Claire needed a clear starting point to help her create a job objective that was personally meaningful. I suggested that she check in with people who knew and respected her to provide a much-needed outside perspective on her capabilities. This is because coming from a stifling work environment, Claire lacked the confidence to recognize her own value.

Claire took the advice and asked friends, colleagues, managers, and family members to recall a time they had seen her at her best, identifying the specific strengths that they had noticed her use in each situation. Everyone who responded remarked on Claire's ability to skillfully coach and counsel people grappling with difficult life situations, whether in their careers or through personal challenges. Her peers commented on her talent in looking beyond superficial aspects of these situations to hear what the person truly needed or wanted. Many talked about changes they had made in their own lives as a result of Claire's meaningful feedback.

When Claire read the compelling comments, she felt that she could at last honor the interest she had always had in becoming a leadership coach. She decided to apply to an executive coaching program. A year later, she had left her spirit-draining position, graduated from the coaching program, and started working in her new vocation.

There's a lesson here for all of us in Claire's story: while you may fear your negative emotions at work because you're worried about losing control, being socially rejected, or simply don't like feeling bad, negative states send you an important message. They alert you to the fact that something in your professional life needs your immediate attention. People tend to assign definitive value judgments to feelings—positive feelings like happiness, hope, gratitude, confidence, enthusiasm, and joy are "good," while negative feelings like frustration, fear, anger, guilt, sadness, anxiety, stress, envy, and loneliness are "bad." But in reality, feelings are neither all good nor all bad. Once you understand this concept, you can learn how to effectively harness your "darker" emotions to bring positive change to your career. The exercise below will give you a starting point for approaching your negative feelings at work more strategically.

EXERCISE A: NEGATIVE EMOTION ASSESSMENT

The first step in learning how to use your negative emotions strategically is recognizing them. Are you so accustomed to squelching your more uncomfortable emotions at work that you find yourself in situations where you're not even sure *what* you're feeling? If you were brought up to believe that expressing certain emotions is a sign of weakness, then ignoring or minimizing your negative feelings may seem normal to you. But one of the main reasons you have emotions is to help you evaluate your experiences to affect your future decisions.

The following exercise is designed to help you understand where you fall on the spectrum of recognizing and accepting your "dark side." For each question, pick the answer that most closely matches how you feel the majority of the time:

1. You have a good understanding of what you're feeling, particularly when you're upset.
    a. Rarely
    b. Usually

2. You're able to accept and express your emotions even when they're unpleasant.
    a. Rarely
    b. Usually

3. When you feel angry, you tend to:
    a. Tell yourself it's not that important and try not to think about it.
    b. Acknowledge the feeling and try to understand where it comes from.

4. When you make a mistake at work, you usually:
    a. Feel ashamed and worry that you might lose your job.
    b. Feel badly but accept your mistake and try to learn from it.

5. Your co-worker blows up at you for something you forgot to do. You:
   a. Blame yourself for making a silly mistake.
   b. Feel hurt by your colleague's yelling and wait for him/her to calm down.

6. When you experience anger, you:
   a. Feel guilty.
   b. Know that it's temporary.

7. How often do you regret past actions?
   a. Frequently
   b. Not often

8. If you have to deal with someone who pushes your buttons at work, you:
   a. Avoid the person and distract yourself from how you feel.
   b. Do your best to understand how your co-worker makes you feel and why.

9. If your manager unfairly criticizes your performance, you tend to:
   a. Feel hurt but let it go.
   b. Set up a meeting to discuss how you feel and why.

If you chose "a" for most of the questions, then you may be trying too hard to suppress your unpleasant feelings, which could lead to more stress in the long run. Remind yourself that uncomfortable feelings are just as important as positive ones in helping you make sense of your career's ups and downs so that you can navigate through them more successfully. If you answered "b" to the majority of questions, then you have a healthy relationship with your emotions. Use this self-awareness to help you identify when you need to make changes in your work life.

A LITTLE GUILT IS A GOOD THING

Remember back in Chapter 4 when I shared how my then-sales manager called me one Sunday morning to chastise me about a client who was publically berating my sales team on the front page of the business section of the newspaper? When that happened, I was wracked with shame. The fact was that I had struggled for months to figure out how to meet the needs of this client while simultaneously juggling many other priorities. Despite the fact that I knew I had done my best with what felt at the time like an impossible situation, I sunk into gloom about the mishap, blaming myself for the outcome.

Looking back on this time in my career with a new awareness about the value of negative emotions, it's now clear that I had a choice of how to react—and I'm not talking about feeling positive instead of feeling negative. I'm talking about choosing which *type* of negative reaction to have in response to a difficult situation. I could have been angry that I never received the appropriate training that would have prepared me to deal with a manipulative client in a complex account. I could have felt guilty over my flawed response that led to my customer's reaction. Or I could have wallowed in shame. I chose shame, believing that I had no control over what happened to me. After the incident, my management did little to dispel the notion that I was not up to the task of being a sales manager of a multi-million-dollar account. Telling me that I had to fix the situation without offering support or guidance only served to reinforce my shame.

What I came to realize after talking with colleagues and friends is that at the age of 25, I did not have the experience to manage a highly politicized environment and because of my lack of proficiency, I could not have done better than I did at that time. This understanding enabled me to eventually let go of the shame. Once I did so, I felt motivated to find a way to improve my relationship with my disgruntled client. I developed creative strategies to rebuild a better relationship with her and eventually succeeded.

In hindsight, I can see that feeling temporarily guilty for my role in the situation would have been a healthier response than sinking into shame. That's because there is a profound difference between guilt and shame, although we often think of them as interchangeable. While not always accurate, guilt sometimes is the result of doing something that doesn't reflect the values or standards you hold for yourself. Shame, on the other hand, is simply about feeling worthless and unchangeable.

Keep this subtle distinction in mind the next time you make a mistake at work. Pay attention to your reactions—your feelings, body sensations, and thoughts—and try to identify whether you are associating your perceived error with a feeling of guilt, or of shame. If shame is the overriding feeling, see if you can shift your emotional response. The exercise below can help you get a clearer sense of your specific reactions at work so that you can start to steer them rather than letting them steer you.

TRY THIS

You might be surprised by how quickly you try to dismiss, reject, fear, minimize, or ignore your negative emotions and thus miss out on the opportunity for tapping into their potential to guide you. Think back to a time when you made a mistake at work and felt guilty—or worse yet ashamed. The incident you choose should have taken place at least a year ago to give you sufficient time to gain perspective. Perhaps a customer threatened to take their business elsewhere, or a project you were leading ended up behind schedule. Maybe an initiative you spearheaded did not have the impact you hoped it would have. After thinking about the specifics of what occurred, answer the following questions:

1. What was the specific project/situation, and what outcome did you expect?

    _____

    _____

2. How did you react immediately after the disappointment? Was your response primarily one of guilt, or of shame?

    _____

    _____

3. How did your manager respond to what happened?

    _____

    _____

4. How did you feel one year after the setback? Was there any change in how you felt about it compared to immediately after? If so, what changed?

    _____

    _____

5. What might have produced a better outcome?

    _____

    _____

6. Was the failure completely beyond your control?

    _____

    _____

7. Looking back on the situation, what did you learn from it?

    _____

    _____

8. Did this experience motivate you to make a change in how you were working? If so, what did you change?

_____

_____

9. Did you take any steps to prevent a similar situation from occurring? If so, what steps did you take?

_____

_____

10. In reflecting on this situation, how did your perspective change over time?

_____

_____

Regardless of the type of emotions you felt during and after this situation, this exercise should help you see the value of your negative feelings—try to use this awareness to tap into their potential for guidance. As difficult as it was at the time, such emotions may have been driving factors in helping you make positive changes that you might not have considered had your career been sailing along smoothly.

ANGER—IT'S WHAT YOU DO WITH IT THAT COUNTS

Do you believe that anger is a dangerous emotion that's risky to express? Anger can be a useful emotion when channeled appropriately, yet it's probably the one feeling that people are most hesitant to call on in a work environment. An angry response does need to be thoughtfully managed. But when used with restraint, it can help you assertively respond to distressing political situations at work, as well as times when you feel you've been wronged, or when the well-being of a colleague is threatened.

Expressing anger cautiously is crucial to maintaining professionalism. Yet treading too lightly when responding to something that upsets you can have consequences as well, since no one wants to feel bullied. So what is the right way to show anger at work? Can you recall situations when a manager in your organization expressed intense displeasure without going too far—or on the flip side went overboard? What did you notice in each case? It's a delicate balance—you don't want to earn the reputation of being unpleasant or argumentative, yet if you have a legitimate reason for feeling angry, it's important to express your concerns—as long as you can do so constructively.

Let's take the example of Mike, one of my coaching clients. Mike complained that he was frequently being left out of important meetings and not copied on critical emails within his department, making him angry. In the absence of explanation, Mike concocted all types of conspiracy theories, convincing himself that his job was at risk. He felt angry, scared, and confused. I encouraged Mike to end the guessing game and talk with his boss. "What's the best way to approach him," he asked? I suggested that he state the facts as he saw them, leaving the emotion out and focusing instead on how being in the loop would enable him to make a greater contribution to the team. "Let's practice now," I encouraged as a way to give Mike the opportunity to try out his wording in a safe situation.

The first two times that Mike tried to practice with me what he wanted to say to his boss, he flushed with anger and his voice rose. By the third practice round, however, he felt calmer and was able to convey his concerns in a reasonable way. Feeling empowered, Mike set up a meeting with his boss and was surprised by the outcome. Instead of getting defensive, Mike's manager quickly apologized and admitted that omitting Mike from critical communications was a result of being hasty, not deliberate. Mike's manager also promised to make a greater effort not to let this type of oversight happen again.

When you repress your anger, your feelings don't just disappear. They are still lurking there beneath the surface and can suddenly come spilling out at an unexpected moment, perhaps misdirectedly. You might be left not knowing why you're so angry since it happens at a time that seems disconnected from the original event, while the recipient of your blast might end up feeling alienated and lose trust in you. You might also wind up physically ill or mentally burned out, so it's important to recognize your triggers and not stuff down your feelings.

With Mike's example in mind, these strategies can help you productively let people know how you feel:

- **Be honest.** Explain up front that you are experiencing strong emotions and that bringing up the subject you want to discuss is hard for you. This prepares the other person or group for a difficult conversation, rather than catching them off-guard or blindsiding them.

- **Slow things down.** If you feel your blood boiling and know that you won't be able to rationally express your thoughts at that moment, it's best to wait. Take a time out if necessary and walk away from the situation to regain control and composure rather than exploding. Suggest to the other parties that a specific time be scheduled to discuss the issue.

- **Think about presentation.** Express your feelings in a respectful, mindful way rather than a classic angry outburst, since the former is more likely to result in the outcome you desire. Getting in someone's face, yelling, or being intimidating is unlikely to lead to a positive response.

- **Avoid expressing rage.** Remember, anger is not the same as rage. Rage is an uncontrollable, sometimes violent form of anger that is not appropriate under any circumstances in the workplace. When vented at others, rage is much more intense and potentially damaging than other milder forms of anger like irritation and frustration. If you do feel rage at work, it's important to walk away from the situation and let yourself cool down. Once you're thinking clearheadedly again, try to recognize what triggered your rage. Understanding what specific circumstances push your buttons can be a useful source of emotional information that can help you shift your attention, thinking, and behavior, ultimately leading to positive outcomes.

ANXIETY: YOUR INTERNAL WARNING SYSTEM

Have you ever worked with someone who was always pointing out what might go wrong? Did it drive you nuts hearing all of the potential pitfalls described in detail when you felt satisfied with the progress you'd made? When I worked in a university career center, I had a colleague whom I fondly referred to as "The Alarm." At almost every staff meeting, The Alarm would caution our team about possible disasters that could occur with everything from our career-fair registration system to our job-posting method. The Alarm's warnings about details and processes that could go kablooey at any moment made me crazy, since I'm a big-picture person by nature.

Despite my personal discomfort with anticipating bad news, I learned a valuable lesson from The Alarm's prophecies: that there's a place for anxiety in the office. Truth be told, she was right about 90 percent of the time, and the alerts she broadcast helped our team prevent problems that could have negatively affected our relationships with clients and students alike.

Research also shows that when CEOs are overly optimistic, they take on more risky debt, putting their companies in jeopardy.[1] Similarly, when entrepreneurs don't anticipate setbacks, their companies bring in less revenue.[2] From these findings, we can conclude that overly confident CEOs, entrepreneurs, and employees alike need to be cautious about falling in love with their ideas, failing to seek feedback that could be helpful, and overlooking the details that can lead to failure.

TRY THIS

Think of anxiety as your early warning system at work, telling you to pay attention to something you might have otherwise glossed over. If you notice yourself regularly feeling anxious before you head to the office, instead of trying to ignore it, stop and ask yourself these three questions:

- What am I feeling?
- What is making me feel this way?
- What can I do about it?

Keep in mind that the type of anxiety we're referring to is more moderate and situation-specific—before a big presentation, performance review, or project deadline when the stakes are temporarily high. This occasional worry is not an all-consuming anxiety that impacts your ability to function day to day. If you experience a higher level of anxiety on an ongoing basis, seek professional guidance from your doctor or a therapist.

LEARNING THAT FEAR IS A LIAR

Almost everyone is familiar with feeling fear about some situations at work. Fear is a biological reaction that has its roots in basic survival. Just because wild animals no longer threaten us on a daily basis doesn't mean that our emotions have kept pace with the comforts of the modern workplace. Fear of natural calamities has been replaced by fear of being judged and rejected by others or of failing at work. While these fears are in seemingly different spheres, their psychological impact is the same in how you experience the emotion physically and mentally.

While fear has a protective role in helping you protect yourself from danger, it can also hold you back. Like its companion "negative" emotions including anger and anxiety, fear provides useful career information if you're willing to read between the lines and hear the message. The problem is when our fear prevents us from making the leap from what we want to do and actually doing it. The more clearly and calmly you can articulate the origins of what you feel afraid of so that you can think about it consciously, the less your fears at work will be able to control you.

To see an example of how succumbing to fear can hold you back in the workplace, consider my client Roy's situation. Devastated by not receiving an offer for a job he wanted, Roy admitted that when asked by the interviewer about his greatest weakness, he had responded: "I'm not assertive." After completing the interview, the employer told Roy: "We have no doubt that you can do the job, but we can't hire someone who doesn't speak up." I asked Roy whether he lacked assertiveness all the time or only in specific situations. He clarified that he only failed to assert himself in staff meetings. "Why?" I asked. "My manager is highly critical of us in meetings, and it's so humiliating to be publically berated," he explained. What Roy may not have realized is that his silence in team meetings was created from fear. Until Roy learns to overcome his fears and address his boss's behavior to get his voice heard, he'll continue to perceive himself as an unassertive person, and others will too.

In a review of multiple studies, [3] researchers found that many employees do not speak up about an issue or concern—or even offer suggestions and ideas—for fear of some type of retaliation on the part of their management. The researchers also emphasize that many managers mistakenly use fear and intimidation as a tactic to motivate performance, not realizing that it actually has the opposite effect—as in Roy's case. More self-aware leaders understand the power of fear and how communicating their own fear or threatening others might have had deleterious consequences, but Roy's manager did not. Roy's silence in the face of an intimidating manager is an all too common scenario—one in which the fear of looking foolish, experiencing isolation, or being embarrassed prevents employees from suggesting changes that could benefit their organization and career. Staying silent, they often sabotage their own advancement.

Insensitive managers aren't always to blame for stoking the flames of fear, however. It's possible to do it to yourself too by believing that your accomplishments and achievements are not good enough. Back in Chapter 1, we discussed how undue self-criticism leads many people to feel like imposters in their careers, fearing exposure for their imagined lack of expertise. Self-sabotaging impostors set excessively high and unrealistic goals, then experience self-defeating thoughts and behaviors when they can't reach those impossible goals. Impostors are driven by the belief that they are currently not good enough, but could do better if only they worked harder.

If you think your own actions and attitudes might be contributing to the fear factor in your life, here are some suggestions for managing fear at work:

- **Recognize your fear.** The first step in overcoming fear is to notice it's there. Think about messages you may have received from parents or teachers that resulted in you having a skewed vision of your success or failure. With this in mind, consider ways you may self-sabotage yourself in your career, such as procrastinating or turning down opportunities for higher visibility.

- **Identify your roadblocks.** Once you've acknowledged your fear, it's time to pay attention to what's getting in the way. Are you hesitant to start a business because you need health insurance? Are you procrastinating about asking for a promotion for fear that your boss may turn you down? Understand that your reasons are excuses, as valid as they may be. Instead of letting them stop you, ask yourself how you can work around them.

- **Prepare.** Roy was able to eventually overcome his fear of speaking up in staff meetings by preparing in advance. He would anticipate the questions his manager was likely to ask, then formulate and practice his answers before the meeting. This built his confidence and thus helped him reduce his fear of potentially being criticized.

- **Broaden your perspective.** The higher you climb in an organization, the more difficult it is to ask for help. Recently appointed CEOs or senior executives frequently believe that they need to know it all. Joining a CEO roundtable or forming a personal board of directors with executives from other companies can help you determine if the goals you set for yourself are realistic.

- **Focus on others.** Imagine that you will be giving a presentation to a group of respected colleagues. You want to make a good impression, but getting up in front of large groups terrifies you. To help calm your nerves, take the spotlight off your fears. Instead of focusing on yourself, think of the information you want to convey and how it will benefit your audience.

- **Take action.** Set aside one day a week as a "courage day," and pick an activity that scares you. The activity needn't be anything as intense as bungee jumping or rock climbing. It can be something small like committing to making one comment at a meeting where you typically remain silent. It might be volunteering to be part of a team for a new project when you tend to focus on contributing individually. The key is that the goal needs to be meaningful to you, and challenging enough that you feel a sense of accomplishment when it is complete.

The problem with succumbing to a need for social acceptance is that it can inhibit you from being courageous, which can hold you back from career success. The pressure you feel to appear smart, successful, and admired can cause you to avoid risks and act too conservatively with career decisions. But while you want to manage your fear, recognize that in small doses, it can be a healthy emotion. Fear can prevent you from engaging in behaviors that are too risky and can jeopardize your career. The trick is to use the strategies above to start to recognize the difference between over-management and under-management of your own personal fear factor.

THE BENEFITS OF STRESS

Are you stressed out? This common question hints at the dangers associated with chronic stress: heart attacks, sleeplessness, depression, and anxiety. The pervasive belief in our culture is that all stress is detrimental and best avoided whenever possible. A recent Internet search on the phrase "avoiding stress" turned up more than 74 million citations. In a 2014 survey, 85 percent of respondents reported believing that stress negatively impacts health, work, and family life.[4]

But from an evolutionary perspective, humans are wired to respond to stress so that we can face danger head-on and survive. How then can such a remarkably adaptive response have gotten such a bad rap? The truth is that stress means different things to different people. You might feel stressed out about a traffic jam, while someone else uses the downtime to enjoy listening to classical music.

Keeping in mind anxiety's role as an early warning system, research has shown that individuals can harness stressful feelings and tap into them to create motivation for proactive problem-solving by anticipating and planning for possible options.[5] (The type of stress I'm referring to is not chronic and long-term; it's situational stress, when you feel that you have some control over the outcome.) When channeled properly, this more temporary, episodic stress response can be beneficial, positioning your brain and body optimally to perform well at work.

The reality is that stress is a factor in everyday life. You have bills to pay and the pressures of being wired 24x7, not to mention perhaps caring for children or aging parents while holding down a job, and any number of other daily stressors. But as you've seen throughout this book, you have the power to alter your mindset, and research shows this is true of your perception of stress as well. In one study,[6] subjects were shown short videos about stress. One group viewed a video about the negative impact of stress. A second group saw a video about the enhancing nature of stress. Participants in the "enhancing" group reported improved psychological symptoms and better work performance, while their colleagues in the "debilitating" group did not. The study proved that the mindset with which you approach stress has a direct effect on your ability to use it to your advantage. Despite these clear results, the media often ignores the enhancing nature of stress.

Other research supports findings that stress builds our brainpower rather than destroys it. For example, a study conducted at University of California at Berkeley showed that moderate, short-lived stress can improve alertness and performance, as well as boost memory.[7] The scientists showed that stress helped monkeys generate new brain cells and bolster their ability to learn and remember. Under the right circumstances, the researchers believe that humans can experience similar benefits.

With this in mind, imagine that you're about to enter an office for a job interview. You feel the usual butterflies in your stomach and racing heartbeat. But what if instead of focusing on your nervousness, you were given instructions by a trusted colleague to think about how getting this job would enable you to help others or contribute to a larger mission aligned with one or more of your core values? Keeping this good advice at the top of mind, during the interview, you noticed that you seemed to be connecting well with the interviewers and that your jitters quickly subsided. The conversation seemed to flow easily, and the interviewers were smiling and speaking as if you already worked there. In fact, the feedback you received from the recruiter is that your answers were more inspiring than those from the other candidates. Let's practice this technique now so you can use it in your next stressful job situation.

TRY THIS

You can train yourself to shift your mindset about stress. When you find yourself facing a career challenge, practice the steps below to give yourself a greater sense of control and empowerment:

- **Think back to your list of values.** Find ways to remind yourself how the challenge you're facing helps meet your deepest values.

- **Shift your focus.** When you find yourself feeling anxious and worrying what others will think of your performance, redirect your attention toward the problem you are trying to solve or how your challenge will help others.

- **Remember past victories.** This isn't the first time in your life that you've beat your stress. Think about some previous occasions when you initially felt stressed but succeeded.

EXERCISE B: STRESS EVALUATION: CHALLENGE OR THREAT?

Now let's take a few minutes to tap into your personal experiences with stress at work. Consider a nerve-racking career or job situation that's affecting you currently. After bringing the specifics of the situation to mind, answer the following questions:

1. What is the situation you are facing?

    _____
    _____
    _____

2. What's makes this situation stressful?

    _____
    _____
    _____

3. Do you have the skills and resources to complete this task?

    _____
    _____
    _____

4. Which of your strengths can you bring to bear?

    _____
    _____
    _____

5. Whose support do you have in this endeavor?

    _____
    _____
    _____

6.   How have you prepared for similar challenges in the past?

       _____

       _____

       _____

7.   When have you felt stressed in the past, and how did you use it to your advantage to achieve a goal?

       _____

       _____

       _____

Review your answers and see if your descriptions suggest that you see your current situation as a challenge, or as a threat. As noted earlier, how you evaluate your ability to handle a difficult situation influences your actual performance under pressure. Whether you view a stressful situation as a challenge or a threat links directly to your ability to follow through successfully. Don't become so concerned that stress is harmful that you overlook the fact that you have successfully overcome challenges in the past by managing your number-one resource: your stress response.

Remember that trying to rid yourself completely of stress and anxiety is likely to make you feel more stressed and anxious; so too for other so-called negative emotions. Owning and learning to maximize the full spectrum of your feelings can help you overcome the inevitable challenges that come hand-in-hand with work and life. As we move into Part III of the book, you'll learn some advanced tips and strategies to sharpen your ability to control your career destiny. In the next chapter, we'll explore how recognizing and seeking out experiences of flow can move your career forward toward greater alignment with your authentic needs and interests.

Part Three

RE-ENGAGE

EIGHT

Harnessing Your Career Energy

"What's your purpose?" asked the instructor. "Write a brief statement about it that you can state easily." I was taking a class on defining your personal brand, and crafting a mission statement was one of my assignments. This should have been a no-brainer for me, since on a daily basis, I help clients discover their brand. My passion is to lead others to create the best version of themselves and create a plan to move from surviving to thriving in their careers. Yet when I had to put the essence of my career aspiration in writing, I struggled, as do many of my clients.

If you can relate, read on. It's time to get closer to your authentic career purpose by looking back on accomplishments that had particular meaning to you. By recognizing when you've had peak career experiences, you'll learn how to recognize what types of activities lead to your "flow states"—times when you feel intensely energized and inspired.

LOOKING FOR SIGNS

Uncovering what you were meant to do rarely happens in a flash. While a handful of people recognize their calling from an early age, they are the rare exceptions. Clients often reach out to me when they've reached a crossroads in their careers. What made them happy when they were in their twenties and thirties is different at age 40 or 50.

Many people hope to discover one central thing that they're "meant" to do in their lives, but the concept of purpose can be broader than that. While it may be unrealistic to assume that your entire life boils down to a single mission, you can look for signs that suggest you're on track toward an authentic career path that really fits. The start of gaining this insight is to tune in to what moves you the most.

If you seek patterns, similarities, or themes in the career choices you've made to date rather than seeing your decisions as a series of disjointed events, you may find some clues about your career purpose. For example, I've had four distinct careers: the first in musical performance, the second in high-technology sales, the third in business development/executive education, and the fourth as a career coach. The thread that ties these seemingly disparate experiences together is my passion for communicating with—and positively impacting—others.

Another way you can mine your past career path for valuable insight is to notice if any previous choices didn't fit with your temperament or fulfill your passion—they didn't bring you into a state of flow. Excelling at your work is not synonymous with career happiness. My client Chris is an example of someone who was outstanding at what he did for a living, yet his work drained rather than energized him. When I first met Chris, he was puzzled by why he felt exhausted at the end of each workday. He genuinely believed in the mission of his organization—providing financing for affordable housing—so he was perplexed as to why he felt so uninspired.

When working with Chris, the first thing we did together was rule out environmental and cultural factors by breaking his job down into specific components that we could isolate and evaluate. By doing so, we confirmed that his lethargy was not related to a miserable boss or unpleasant working conditions. In fact, through this process, we discovered some positives: he liked his colleagues and manager, his hours were manageable, and his commute was short. Next we investigated the job itself. Chris found the work repetitive, and even more frustrating was the fact that his position didn't enable him to build long-term relationships because it was transactional in nature. His passion, on the other hand, was to develop deep client relationships, which he had done earlier in his career. If your job itself drains your energy, that is a clear sign that you might benefit from a career shift to something that allows you to get into your zone, groove, or flow.

FINDING FLOW:
A CLUE TO UNDERSTANDING YOUR PURPOSE

While your past career decisions may provide some insight into a central mission or purpose, they may not provide all of the fodder you need for this level of deep self-discovery. If your review of past career choices fails to illuminate what you truly love to do, another more intrinsic way of listening to your life is to reflect on specific experiences you've had both inside and outside of work. In such moments, you may have been so absorbed by an activity that you lost all sense of time passing. You felt energized, inspired, and capable of accomplishing almost anything—like you were tapping into your true talents and strengths to effortlessly complete the task. Psychologists describe such experiences as "flow states." Flow requires a mindset of concentration and engagement that you can only achieve when you're completing a task that challenges your skills, not when you're swinging in a hammock or relaxing in front of the TV.

Renowned psychologist Mihaly Csikszentmihalyi coined the term "flow."[1] Since the activities that create flow are intrinsically rewarding, the more you experience flow, the more you'll want to do it again, which can help you feel more engaged and fulfilled at work. To understand this concept better, think of skiing down a double black diamond mountain (a very tough course) in the Colorado Rockies or the Swiss Alps. Perhaps you've attempted this particular run before, but this time you feel more mastery than you did in the past: you feel "in the zone." Your experience this time is that your skill level matches the challenge of this difficult slope, and you are elated as you carve each turn and master each mogul. You have a heightened sense of mastery and pride in your achievement. Flow may be involved, resulting in what some describe as a "peak experience."

While it might be easier to come up with favorite sports or hobbies that bring you into a flow state, if you think about it, you may realize that you've had similar experiences in job-related activities. Perhaps you were working heads-down on a particularly challenging but rewarding project, or speaking at a conference on a topic that you've mastered and believe in. These are moments when you forget yourself and begin to act effortlessly, with a heightened sense of awareness of the here and now. A flow experience at work may even come from something as simple as communicating with your team.

TRY THIS

Sometimes understanding your past career choices isn't enough to help you recognize your authentic career path. If this is true for you, then spend some time reflecting on experiences you've had—either personally or professionally—when you became completely absorbed and inspired by the activity itself. When you completed the activity, you might have been surprised by how much time had passed—you were so "in the zone" that you weren't focused on how long the task was taking. Make a list below of any such moments of "flow" that you've experienced. Refer back to this list as you read this chapter, as it may contain valuable insights to guide you closer toward a career mission and purpose that makes sense exclusively for you.

_____

_____

_____

_____

_____

With this list of your flow-inducing activities, you have some important clues that can help in determining your career mission. One caveat: it's important to note that the experience of flow, while intense, is transient. You should not expect flow experiences to be constant. What's most important is to understand the _conditions_ that put you in a flow state and learn how to recreate them.

HOW TO GET INTO THE FLOW

Now that you've had a chance to test some of your peak experiences for flow potential, you may be wondering how you can consciously tap into this potential more often. Here are some strategies designed to bring you back to your own "double black diamond" moments again and again:

- **Seek your "sweet spot."** Since flow experiences require that a high challenge meets your high level of skill to reach the challenge, your focus should be on finding the intersection between them considering your interests, skills, and strengths. For example, designing a new marketing program from the ground up may motivate someone who is highly skilled in marketing but may have previously only had the opportunity to manage a few aspects of a marketing function. Alternatively, for someone else whose top skills are in operations and finance, it may be more energizing to design new processes such as financial reports or automate formerly manual tasks for greater efficiencies. Remember we discussed earlier that people are more engaged in their work when their goals are self-motivated rather than defined by others. So to find your professional sweet spot that leads to flow, you need both the skills to do the job *and* to believe in the value of the work itself.

- **Clarify your goals.** It's much easier to lose yourself in an activity if you know what's expected of you and what will constitute success. Therefore, as you work toward pinpointing your professional mission, be sure that you've identified clear goals. The goals that keep a lawyer motivated might include not just winning the case, but also researching similar cases, building a defense strategy, and encouraging the client. Similarly, for a research scientist, developing a medicine that can make it into clinical trials and clear regulatory hurdles to become a marketed product to relieve pain is only one part of the equation. Other goals might include collaborating with industry experts, developing research techniques that could lead to a better clinical outcome, and finding workarounds for stubborn problems. We'll talk more about goal setting in Chapter 11.

- **Focus on the process.** In my work as a career coach, I've noticed that people often miss the opportunity to experience flow because they focus too much on the end result and not enough on the process of reaching their goals at work. While the end game may certainly be important, what happens along the way is often the locus of a meaningful experience. Think about where the gratification of finding a new job comes from, for example—from getting the offer, or from convincing the employer that you're the best person for the job and negotiating your terms? While the job offer itself is certainly satisfying, I've seen many clients feel deeper reward from their ability to successfully influence the process that *leads* to the desired outcome. In Chapter 2, we discussed that happiness can come from enjoying the journey of reaching your goal no matter what the outcome is, and this applies to flow as well. What matters most for entering flow is the *quality of the experience* while doing the activity regardless of the result.

- **Look within for feedback.** To be able to immerse yourself in an activity, it helps to know that the work matters to your colleagues, supervisors, or clients. But even more important is if you intrinsically value the work and are able to access the feedback that comes from doing it. For example, if you're giving a presentation, you can glean audience response by reading facial expressions and body language, as well as by listening to their questions and comments. But the higher the level of mastery you feel as a speaker, the better you'll be able to evaluate your own performance in real time. This ability to trust your internal responses rather than external ones—based on your own knowledge and experience—is crucial for entering flow.

- **Block out interruptions.** People in a flow state experience intense concentration, which gives them the ability to block out distractions to focus on the task at hand. In today's work environment where we are barraged with emails, phone calls, and text messages practically 24x7, multi-tasking is a necessary evil, making it nearly impossible to concentrate for more than a short period at a superficial level. Keep in mind that when you're frequently distracted by new and different tasks, shifting from one to another, it makes it tough to enter the flow zone. Minimizing multi-tasking and setting aside blocks of time to focus on jobs that require effort and concentration will afford the right conditions to enter a flow state.

EXERCISE A:
EVALUATING YOUR POTENTIAL TO FIND FLOW

To understand whether or not your current job situation is conducive to entering a flow state, it's important to shine a light on your work culture—as well as on your own thinking and choices related to your tasks. They will help you understand if your work environment and how you spend your time at work offer the ideal conditions for flow to arise, or if these factors may keep your potential for flow at bay.

1. I have the ability at work, for the most part, to decide what to pay attention to and how to prioritize my time.
    a. True
    b. False

2. My goals are clear and measurable—I understand how my success is measured.
    a. True
    b. False

3. My management supports my work, and I receive unambiguous feedback about my performance.
    a. True
    b. False

4. I receive regular feedback from my peers and manager.
    a. True
    b. False

5. My work challenges me in a good way.
    a. True
    b. False

6. My work enables me to craft my job to my strengths.
   a. True
   b. False

7. I have time during my workweek to think about the problems I'm trying to solve and discuss them with my colleagues.
   a. True
   b. False

8. I find joy in the work that I do.
   a. True
   b. False

9. My work provides challenging opportunities that let me use the skills I have honed over time, balancing challenges with my skills.
   a. True
   b. False

10. Collaboration is encouraged where I work.
    a. True
    b. False

If you answered "True" to most or all of the questions, then you most likely have opportunities to experience flow in your work and seek out opportunities to find more. If you answered "False" to most or all of the questions, you may be relying too heavily on preconceived ideas about how you think you're supposed to accomplish your work. This could be a sign that your self-critical tendencies are hampering your willingness to propose new and potentially more satisfying ways to achieve your goals and experience flow more often. On the other hand, if you've tried talking to your manager about novel approaches to your job only to be told that they want things done the company's way, then your current environment may not be a good fit with your strengths, skills, and interests—and it may be time to move on.

THE FLOW OF CURIOSITY

In *Creativity: The Psychology of Discovery and Invention*,[2] a sequel to Csikszentmihalyi's book on flow, the author profiles individuals including scientists, poets, artists, mathematicians, musicians, rock climbers, and chess players who devote time to a pursuit regardless of whether they earn a living or recognition doing it. What he learned is that these people share common experiences of practicing challenging, often difficult activities that require skill mastery, which they found inherently rewarding. Regardless of the activity that produced it or the recognition they did or didn't receive, these "experts" at their chosen craft explain their experiences in almost identical ways as being in the moment, totally absorbed, in the zone.

Back in Chapter 1, we discussed that a narrow definition of creativity—one in which some people are genetically more gifted than others—is born of perfectionism. This erroneous belief may lead you to adhere to a false career identity that keeps you locked into a limited range of thinking and behaving. The above study of creative lives can be applied to anyone who wants to shed their false career persona, explore a more authentic work-self, and experience more instances of flow.

Let's put this research-based information about flow and creativity into a more personal context. I previously mentioned my client, Marie. I first met Marie when she hired me to help her strategize the best way to grow her consulting business, which was focused on the biotech industry. I must admit, I was skeptical about her ability to break into a field that highly values PhDs and people with specific technological expertise, neither of which Marie possessed. How would someone whose career spanned running operations at Planned Parenthood, to financial planning and reporting, to an organizational development consultant for a semiconductor company build credibility with leaders in such a specialized industry?

But Marie proved me wrong and was successful in reaching her challenging career goals. What I hadn't anticipated were three things: Marie's passion for her new field, her ability to listen intently, and her capacity to draw parallels between situations in different fields and apply them to create solutions to thorny technical problems. Something else I found remarkable in my interactions with Marie was how when she recalled interviews with clients about their challenges, it was as if she was still sitting across from them, mesmerized by the conversation, completely in a flow state.

As her coach, talking to Marie about her area of career passion was like watching the performance of an exceptional athlete or musician. I was spellbound by her openness to take on new challenges without being sure of the outcome, her lack of ego, and her thirst for helping her clients. What can you learn from Marie's experience about flow and creativity, and how to harness them to enhance your own career mission? Here are some strategies that I gleaned from our conversations:

- **Minimize obstacles.** Multitasking is the greatest enemy of creativity—and of flow. Marie allowed herself the opportunity to consider the roadblocks her clients were facing by not rushing to prescribe an immediate solution, instead giving herself the chance to think about a variety of options. Even more striking was that she was not driven by a fear that she might not have all the answers, nor by a need to protect her ego. Almost selfless in her approach, her singular goal was to contribute to something bigger than herself, not to prove her intelligence or savvy. Instead, she saw herself as serving a greater purpose: supporting others in realizing their vision. Can you apply this lesson in your own work—focusing not on your own success but on the greater good—to help you move closer to flow?

- **Awaken curiosity.** Continually trying to prove your worth and avoid mistakes kills creativity, as does buying into the mindset that your capabilities are fixed and can't improve. Marie did not let her lack of formal training in the specific field stop her. Her curiosity led her to learn about her new industry's unique challenges and apply her experience so that she could help improve outcomes. By immersing herself deeply in what she was learning and being willing to experiment creatively, she quickly became invaluable to her new clients.

- **Set goals.** People who prioritize creative responses to their career challenges—like Marie did—know what's meaningful to them and what they want to accomplish. So instead of letting the day define your agenda, pick an activity the night before that is intrinsically interesting to you and add it to your calendar, along with a specific goal. Your goal related to the activity can be relatively minor, such as starting the day by listening to an inspiring podcast on your way to work, or listening to music that your find motivating. What's most important is that the activity energizes you, and that setting goals related to your authentic interests becomes a habit.

- **Make time for relaxation.** Our culture highly values busyness. The more we pile on in a day, the more we can pat ourselves on the back—or so we think. The truth is that constant busyness is another creativity killer. There are times when you need to recharge your batteries and get away from work. Marie took the time she needed—including downtime—to figure out the best strategic approach to her new business. Creativity can't be directed on a schedule.

- **Prime your space.** Your physical surroundings can have a major influence on flow and creativity. Pay attention to how you feel in different office spaces and working environments. Are you more productive in light-filled rooms? Do family photos or favorite quotes remind you of your values and accomplishments? The type of setting you choose to work in—as well as the things you surround yourself with—can help or hamper your creativity. Marie kept a book of appreciative emails and thank-you notes she received from clients next to the computer in her office. She frequently reviewed these comments to remind herself of the positive impact that she had on her clients. In her light-filled office, Marie also hung pictures with quotes from people she admired to keep her inspired.

- **Pinpoint pain points.** Creative people like Marie don't rush to a hypothesis or assume they immediately have all the answers. They examine a problem from multiple angles first, considering different causes and testing their assumptions. In Marie's case, she perceived and defined a specific pain point facing people in her new industry: a lack of communication and collaboration. Marie first saw the potential for improving the industry's standard process, and then clearly demonstrated to potential clients how she could help them positively impact their work. Creative people don't adhere to the status quo if they find better ways to solve a problem. What pain points can you identify—and potentially solve—relating to your current projects or clients?

- **Experiment with passion.** A theme we've repeatedly returned to throughout this book is the popular but inaccurate belief that we should know at an early age what career path to follow. The fact is that few of us know right away the fields for which we have a natural affinity, and child prodigies are few and far between. Marie's career fit this pattern in that she did not follow a straight and narrow path to success. Instead, it took considerable time for

146

her to recognize the common themes of improving processes, empowering teams, and facilitating communications that criss-crossed her diverse career spanning nonprofit and technology. It was only after ample experimentation throughout her career with what she did and didn't enjoy that she was able to land on her true vocation.

The daily consistency of practicing these strategies will enable you to more quickly enter flow, and find the activities that provide you with more flow experiences in your job. Armed with these insights, you can consciously seek out these types of activities in your work and other parts of your life. You can ultimately use these findings—combined with the values assessment that you completed in Chapter 6—to help you recognize and pursue your authentic career mission.

In the next chapter, you'll learn how knowing and leveraging the right resources—including time, money, health, and social support—to achieve your goals can also contribute to your career happiness and success. You'll learn to identify personal resources that you may currently have available but may be underutilizing, as well as where and how to find additional support structures that can help maximize your career authenticity.

NINE

Mining Your Personal Resources to Boost Your Career

Just as natural resources are limited, so too are your personal ones. Knowing how to identify and effectively leverage the right resources to help you achieve your professional goals is another key to maximizing your authenticity so you can thrive in your career. Personal resources that you have at your disposal can help you move toward a wide range of possible end goals, whether it's finding more balance, achieving a promotion, negotiating a pay increase, or finding a job in better alignment with your values.

What exactly *are* your personal resources, though, and how can you tap into them at work for maximum advantage? While money might be the first thing to come to mind when you hear the word "resources," often factors that *aren't* related to salary, earnings, or savings can make an even bigger difference in how you feel about your job.

In this chapter, you'll learn to recognize and draw upon several key nonfinancial resources that you may be overlooking: social and professional support, energy, time, and health. By utilizing these resources on a regular basis, you'll be in a better position to thrive in your career regardless of your income level. Let's start by examining what you can gain careerwise when you learn how to build a network of solid community support.

ASSEMBLING YOUR PERSONAL "BOARD OF DIRECTORS"

Four executive women—myself included—gathered around a table and introduced ourselves, sharing our goals and visions. Two of the women were executives in their industries, and two of us agreed to be their mentors to help serve as thinking partners. We had each pledged to embark on a six-month journey during which we would encourage, challenge, and support each other in becoming our best, most authentic selves. As one of the mentors, I was excited about how much we would all learn from each other and what would unfold. Sharing hopes, dreams, setbacks, and advice with others helps build enduring relationships and provides invaluable outside perspectives.

This is the power of identifying and tapping a personal "board of directors" (BoD) to help guide your career path and inform your decisions. As you'll learn more about later in this chapter, your BoD might meet regularly and formally as our executive women's group did, or you might find people for your board with whom you can speak to more informally by phone or email for insight. Either way, identifying trusted others to participate in a board-like capacity for you can produce significant professional dividends.

This was certainly the case with the group in which I participated as a mentor. Four months after we started meeting, Jody, one of the executives, was faced with a difficult decision about whether to stay in her current role or leave it for another opportunity. To complicate matters, Jody also felt perplexed about whether or not she should negotiate employment terms and compensation with her prospective new employer. She worried that if she did try to negotiate—which was necessary to help her make an informed decision about staying or going—she might come across as pushy and demanding. Had Jody not requested input from her BoD, she might have decided against negotiating in order to find out more, and almost certainly would not have attempted to leave her current job to take on the new role. In fact, with her personal board's encouragement, she did both successfully and felt very happy with the results. How did the input from her colleagues affect Jody's decisions, and why were her ultimate guided choices so different than what her fear-based thinking was initially telling her to do?

As we learned earlier, in the face of a major decision, it's easy to fall back on what you already know and believe to be true rather than remaining open to other possibilities. This was definitely true in Jody's case, since she initially identified with the belief that it was paramount to take care of others' needs before her own and avoid being perceived as "high maintenance" by her potential employer. The idea of leaving the staff she had hired and developed at her current company caused her to feel terribly guilty, and in conjunction with that emotion, asking for more than she was offered from a new employer made her nervous about appearing as the stereotype of a "pushy woman."

Yet when sharing her concerns with the group—her personal BoD—we challenged Jody's assumptions, sharing examples of what we had done in similar situations. Our collective feedback empowered Jody with the courage she needed to reexamine her long-held beliefs and make room for new possibilities. Ultimately, listening to her board members resulted in Jody leaving her position and negotiating what she was worth in terms of title, responsibilities, compensation, and benefits.

151

WHO MAKES AN IDEAL BOARD MEMBER?

It may not be easy to figure out who you should ask to be on your personal BoD. Part of the value of a group of mentors lies in their diversity—and in some cases, their distance from your current employer. In certain cases, it can be easier to find an internal mentor who can help you rise through the ranks at your current company. Yet choosing only BoD members from your current firm is not the most strategic choice, since with reorganizations, downsizing, acquisitions, mergers, and business failures, your mentor is just as likely to move on or be laid off from the company as you are. Plus, if you hitch your wagon to one person where you work now, you might even be more likely to lose your job if your mentor does, due to your close affiliation.

So instead of seeking a board of directors exclusively from your current company, it's smart to assemble your group more widely. Your goal should be to identify a group of people from different backgrounds and organizations with whom you can confer regularly for advice and feedback. The personal board members you select ideally will be individuals who are supportive yet have the courage to be honest, and are willing to challenge you when it's in your best interest.

In addition to being from different organizations than your own, the group you assemble might also complement you in the following ways:

- **Industry expertise.** Your board members should have some working knowledge of your industry or the industry you are targeting for transition, even if they are currently working in another industry.

- **Diversity of ideas.** They should be more knowledgeable than you in certain realms of business, offering greater expertise or different points of view.

152

- **Different levels.** It's also helpful for your advisors to have varying levels of experience, which means both industry peers and more senior-level managers/executives can be considered for board inclusion. You might want to invite a former boss, a colleague you admire, or both. If you are a senior manager yourself, consider networking with professionals or consultants who have expertise in your specialty to identify potential BoD members.

- **Generational differences.** With five generations currently in the workforce, it can be valuable to draw on a cross-section of people from different ages and career stages. Consider including younger board members (think Gen Y, Z, or Millennials) alongside Gen Xers and Baby Boomers to elicit wider perspectives.

In some cases, your board might not meet all of the criteria above. As long as there's enough diversity in key areas for members to add value to each other, there's no need to worry about having the full range of possible differences on your board. In our mentoring circle, for example, although we were all at the executive level (even the mentors), we brought varied expertise to the table from a wide range of industries and roles. We also all worked for different organizations, which helped quickly build trust since there was no worry about conflicting interests or allegiances.

It may be impractical to ask your inner circle to meet as a full group face to face, due to logistical difficulties coordinating multiple schedules and locations. If that's the case, prioritize meeting with each of your board members regularly one on one, and be clear about the type of input you are seeking. Give each individual board member all the background and facts needed to get the most out of their experience and advice. Make the investment in taking them out to lunch or dinner for your chats to return the favor whenever possible. There's always the option of communicating by phone or email when schedules don't mesh, but try to make time for at least occasional in-person meetings to build greater rapport.

PERSONAL ENERGY MANAGEMENT

Just like social capital, energy is a valuable resource. Yet while you may be keenly aware of managing your time by meeting deadlines, getting to work on time, squeezing in an extra project, and responding to emails before and after work and on the weekends, you might not be aware of the toll that all of this activity takes on your energy level. And while you may know all too well that time is finite, you may be less conscious of the link between the time you spend on something and how it affects the amount of energy you have each day.

As an example, A 2010 LexisNexis survey[1] of 1,700 white-collar workers in the U.S., China, South Africa, the U.K., and Australia revealed that on average, employees spend more than half their work-days receiving and managing information rather than using it to do their jobs—a huge energy drain. What is the key to replenishing your energy at work? The answer is actively seeking energy renewal through developing healthy daily habits like taking breaks—habits that many companies fail to support or encourage. Ignoring the importance of energy renewal is a mistake, since research clearly shows its value. A study reported in *The New York Times* found that employees who take a break every 90 minutes report a 30 percent higher level of focus than those who take no breaks or just one during the day.[2] The researchers also reported a nearly 50 percent improved ability to think creatively, and a 46 percent higher level of health and well-being, post-break. The more people work beyond 40 hours a week and the more continuously they work, the worse they feel and the less engaged they become. On the other hand, when management encourages people to take breaks, it increases by nearly 100 percent employees' likelihood to stay with any given company while doubling their sense of health and well-being.

Psychologist Anders Ericsson demonstrated that most people can engage in intense work or practice for only 60-90 minutes without taking a break.[3] This includes highly accomplished individuals from different disciplines including music, sports, and writing. In a famous study[4] of young violinists' performance, Ericsson found that the most accomplished performers practiced in the morning, in three increments of no more than 90 minutes each, with a break between each one. Like the violinists, the breaks you build into your workday needn't be very long. Even 5 to 10 minutes to stretch, take a walk around the block, meditate, or listen to music is enough to help you recharge your batteries and return to your work with renewed energy.

VALUING YOUR TIME

The frantic text from my client Jackie's boss came in at 8:00 on a Saturday morning: "The spending projection model is wrong and needs to be fixed immediately." Jackie texted back: "Can this wait until Monday? I have guests visiting from out of town." "The VP wants it," her manager responded curtly. "It will only take you two to three hours."

Feeling pressured, Jackie dropped what she was doing to prepare for her houseguests and shifted gears immediately to work on the financial model for her boss. Certainly, some situations call for an urgent response, but the scenario between Jackie and her boss was not one of them. After all, the spending model was for the following fiscal year and would not impact business in the near-term.

How many times have you been asked to work during your free time when there wasn't a crisis? Part of effective energy management involves learning how to value your own time. Putting a dollar value on your day requires more than dividing your pay by the number of hours that you worked. It requires thinking deeply about the tradeoffs you are willing to make.

Researchers are beginning to look at the value of time in new ways, producing tools and insights that can help you make more sensible choices, and you can do so too. Think about determining a market value for your time by dividing your total compensation by the number of hours you work, or how much you'd be willing to spend on a time-saving tool or service. You might also ponder how much money it would take to get you to give up your free time. You may realize that you actually place a higher value on your free time than your current pay rate. The catch is, do you live by those values?

TRY THIS

If you think that you value your free time more than your current pay rate, test out your hypothesis by asking yourself these three questions:

- If your time is worth $25 per hour, should you spend 30 minutes a week walking to and from the dry cleaner, or should you pay $40 a month to have your cleaning picked up and delivered by a dry-cleaning service?

- If your time is worth $60 per hour, should you always pay $99 a year for shipping, or should you spend one hour a month at a department store?

- If your time is worth $80 per hour, should you always buy the direct flight that saves you two hours, even if it costs $250 more than the flight with a three-hour layover?

Surprised by the answers? Living by your values means putting your money where your mouth is when it comes to taking time for what matters to you. The benefit of calculating time versus money and grading activities you value is that it brings into sharp perspective the discrepancies between how you value your time and how you actually choose to spend it.

You might consider tracking your free time to see how many hours you're using for leisure versus work, but placing a dollar value on your time might create more pressure, especially if you tend to beat yourself up for not working harder. Instead, consider your free time to be non-negotiable, viewing hours earmarked to relax and decompress as a vital personal resource that ultimately enables you to be more efficient during working hours. In essence, you need to value your downtime and leisure activities that add health and wellness to your life as much as time at your desk if you want to thrive in your career.

Here are a few other strategies related to the interdependent resources, time and energy:

- **Obey the law of diminishing returns.** When should you call it quits for the day? Continuing to work on a project only makes sense until you reach the point of diminishing returns. With that in mind, think about times of day that you're able to summon your freshest creative energy and most productive work bursts. Try to schedule your most challenging tasks during these hours, and also notice times that your thinking feels fuzzy and you have a harder time concentrating. There's no point wasting time spinning your wheels unproductively; take a break during your less productive times of the day to maximize your energy output.

- **Rank happiness and meaning.** As you figure out where to dispense your precious and limited time and energy, think about how happiness and meaning figure into the equation. It's something of a no-brainer to designate more hours and energy toward activities that either make you feel better, fill you with a sense of purpose, or both.

157

- **Challenge the myth of macho multi-tasking.** In our amped-up 24x7 world, it often seems like the only way to get though the day is via multi-tasking. The average white-collar employee receives 147 emails a day and spends 28 percent of his or her time responding to them.[5] The problem is, multitasking doesn't help you get work done faster. Research shows that completing tasks takes 24 percent longer when multi-tasking compared with not switching back and forth.[6] Multi-tasking also results in greater errors, higher stress levels, and lower creativity—so just say no to dividing your focus.

- **Doing less drives better results.** If you tend toward perfectionism, you may think that doing more things will help improve your results. It doesn't. Doing things better is what drives results. Truthfully, doing one thing as best you can drives the best results.[7] Although the need to answer emails is not going away any time soon, how you choose to manage your email traffic and other disruptions is largely under your control. For example, instead of reading your emails throughout the day, pick three time-bounded periods during the day to do it. Instead of reading your emails first thing in the morning, prioritize the tasks that will take the most time and attention and do those first, before other distractions get in the way.

PHYSICAL AND MENTAL HEALTH AS PERSONAL RESOURCES

You've started to develop strong social support by creating a personal board of directors, and you are getting good at effectively monitoring your time and energy. Now you can bring it all home by incorporating healthy habits into your workday. Often overlooked as a resource, your physical and mental health can play a significant role in helping you thrive in your career. Here are some strategies to get you going:

- **See physical exercise as part of your job.** The health benefits of physical exercise are no secret. Yet although we often hear about how regular exercise can lower your blood pressure, help with weight control, and decrease your chance of developing illnesses such as heart disease and diabetes, have you embraced physical fitness in your daily life? Over the past decade, compelling evidence has mounted about the mind-body connection, pointing to the benefits of regular exercise on cognitive functioning and well-being. In fact, research indicates that your mental acuity is directly linked to your exercise routine, whether you're older or younger.[8] And nowhere are these implications more relevant than to your performance and ability to thrive at work. Countless studies have revealed a wide range of benefits you can experience as a result of incorporating regular exercise into your routine, including:

  - Improved concentration
  - Sharper memory
  - Faster learning
  - Prolonged mental stamina
  - Enhanced creativity
  - Lower stress

- **Make time for mood maintenance.** Exercise has also been shown to elevate mood, which has beneficial implications for workplace performance and well-being. Since most jobs require building relationships and fostering collaboration, having a positive attitude can influence your degree of success. When you take care of your mental health, it becomes one of the resources available in your toolkit to improve your overall satisfaction with life and work. Researchers have found that when people experience positive emotions, their awareness expands and they can see greater possibilities, resulting in benefits such as increased creativity[9] and better ability to bounce back from adversity.[10]

159

- **Get outdoors.** Spending more time outside in a peaceful setting—whether a park, waterfront, or anywhere neither noisy nor congested—can also decrease mental fatigue. If you can't actually leave your office, even *looking* at the great outdoors can help by spending a few minutes viewing pictures of natural scenery. In a study,[11] researchers asked students to memorize lists of random numbers. They were then asked to recite them from memory in reverse order before completing another attention-demanding task in which they had to remember the locations of certain words arranged in a grid. Half the students subsequently walked in a park for an hour while the other half walked the same distance through highly trafficked streets of a downtown area. The volunteers that walked in nature recalled more numbers than those who had walked through the city.

- **Claim your vacation time.** Over the past 15 years, Americans have reduced the amount of vacation they take by almost a week.[12] If you're one of them, it might interest you to know the potential consequences of relinquishing your annual chance to renew and refresh yourself. One long-term study[13] found that men who don't take vacations are 30 percent more likely to have heart attacks than those who do. For women, it's 50 percent. Women who fail to take vacation are also more likely to suffer from depression.[14] Many people believe if they give and give to their job, they will be more successful, regardless of the consequences to the self. But the evidence does not support this assumption.

- **Value mindfulness and meditation.** Another way to facilitate your mental well-being is through cultivating a state of mindful awareness of your surroundings, and one method to get there is through meditation. So much has been written about meditation that it can seem to be positioned as the cure-all for just about everything—but the fact is that much of the hoopla is warranted.

Research has shown that meditation has positive effects on concentration, memory, and mood.[15] Mindfulness practice was originally an ancient Buddhist meditation technique, but in recent years, it has evolved into a range of approaches. MRI scans show that after just two months of mindfulness practice, the brain's "fight or flight" center, the amygdala, appears to shrink and the prefrontal cortex—associated with higher order brain functions such as awareness, concentration, and decision-making—grows.[16] As a result, many mindfulness practitioners find that they are able to be less emotional and more thoughtful in their response to stressful situations.

- **Notice new things.** Even if you are an infrequent meditator like me, you can still derive the benefits of mindfulness without sitting cross-legged on a cushion. Mindfulness practice can sound intimidating, but it's really as simple as keeping your focus on the present moment and actively noticing new things rather than mentally being somewhere else for your experiences. For example, think about a colleague who grates on your nerves. Instead of automatically moving into a frustrated response, try to find three new things about this "annoying" person that you hadn't paid attention to before. The simple act of not going on autopilot and making the same assumptions you usually make about people and situations may enable you to see things differently. This way of paying attention is an example of mindfulness. It's the act of paying attention to the possibility that things might be different than what you assume. Try the exercise below to help you get the hang of mindfulness meditation.

TRY THIS

Let's practice a few of the things you've learned about shoring up your mental resources. First, to increase the flow of positive emotions throughout your workday, write down three positive things that you experience each day. It could be receiving a morning hug from your child, enjoying a delicious lunch, participating in an inspiring conversation with a friend, or hearing a beautiful song on your way to work. Paying attention to the good helps you train your brain to look for more of it while building a storehouse of positivity.

Next, you now know that mindfulness is a way to become more conscious of your feelings, deliberate about your behavior, and aware of your impact on others. Meditation and noticing new things are two methods that can help you achieve greater mindfulness and maintain a positive outlook. Try these two exercises that practice each strategy:

- Meditation doesn't have to be complicated—in fact, it shouldn't be. Even taking a few minutes to sit quietly while following your breath in and out can produce similar results. Try breathing in to a count of three and out to a count of six. Extending the out breath and slowing your breathing can deepen relaxation. Counting or focusing on one object such as your inhalations/exhalations or a mantra are effective ways to enhance concentration and slow the fight or flight response.

- Think about a situation that bothers you at work. Is there a way you can reframe your perspective to notice something different about it? I'll give you an example of how I learned to notice something different. Remember my former co-worker who I teasingly referred to as "The Alarm?" I explained earlier how she bugged the heck out of me because of how predictably she raised concerns about things that could go wrong. After countless hours of perseverating about how annoying she was, I asked myself, "Is there another way that I could view her behavior?" By shifting my focus to notice how her attention to detail *did* prevent some serious mishaps, I was able to see the value she offered instead of just the nuisance. This doesn't mean that I suddenly wanted to be best friends with her, but my intentionally new perspective gave me an appreciation for the skills she offered the organization, which improved our working relationship.

EXERCISE A: PERSONAL RESOURCE MANAGEMENT

Here's an exercise to help you see how well you manage the range of personal resources that you have available to you. Think about how you spend your time during an average workweek, and then answer the questions below:

1. I take a 20-30 minute break for lunch almost every day.
   a. True
   b. False

2. I leave my desk at lunchtime.
   a. True
   b. False

3. I make it a point to go outside during the workday when it is appropriate to take a break.
   a. True
   b. False

4. I notice when my energy is flagging at work.
   a. True
   b. False

5. When I notice my energy waning, I take a short break.
   a. True
   b. False

6.   I regularly take most or all of the vacation time allotted to me.
     a.   True
     b.   False

7.   I take a night off from reading and answering emails at least once a week.
     a.   True
     b.   False

8.   I exercise at least three times a week.
     a.   True
     b.   False

9.   I make time for family and friends.
     a.   True
     b.   False

10. I ask for advice from people I trust before making a major decision.
     a.   True
     b.   False

11. I read my email first thing in the morning when I get to work.
     a.   True
     b.   False

12. I frequently feel overwhelmed.
     a.   True
     b.   False

13. I rarely use all the vacation time to which I'm entitled.
     a.   True
     b.   False

14. I don't believe in spending extra money to save me time.
    a. True
    b. False

15. I usually eat lunch at my desk when I'm working.
    a. True
    b. False

If you answered "True" to most or all of questions 1-10, and "False" to 11-15, then you have a healthy balance between meeting your needs and doing your best at work. If you responded "False" to 1-10 and "True" to 11-15, then your perfectionism may be tripping you up when it comes to thinking about how you think you're supposed to act at work—and this may be getting in the way of paying attention to your personal needs. If this is the case, then you may want to pay more attention to how you spend your time during the day, and when the balance between your work and your life begins to shift out of kilter. If you don't, you may soon find yourself facing a burnout situation.

In the next chapter, we'll explore what science can teach us about failure, and how to look at disappointments as learning opportunities that can help lead you to better outcomes in the future. You'll also learn strategies for mining your failures for insight that can inform your future career and job choices.

TEN

Treating Failure Like a Scientist

You didn't get the job. You missed the deadline. You didn't ask for help and made a critical error because of it. You made a bad hire. You failed to plan in advance. You said yes to too many things. You forgot something important. You flubbed a presentation. It doesn't matter what the reason is behind not achieving the results you expected or wanted. The truth is that your interpretation of a situation that feels like "failure" can mean the difference between leaning into your authenticity and using it to move toward building the career you want, or getting stuck in self-blame that keeps you from progressing toward your goals.

With this in mind, as you read this chapter, take the opportunity to pause, examine your own approach to failure, and then practice some healthy responses to not getting what you want right away. You'll learn more about possible strategies as you read on and can use the advice to help you focus your attention in four areas:

- Recognizing whether you've been avoiding taking chances because you're afraid that you might fail.

- Embracing risk-taking as an intentional way to build courage and resilience.

- Realizing that not every project will be successful from the onset, and not every solution will be easy to discover.

- Noticing that if you give yourself permission to fail, you will build courage, resilience, and grit.

WHAT MIGHT YOU MISS OUT ON BY GIVING UP TOO SOON?

A recent Google search on "fear of failure" yielded more than 50 million results. The popularity of this search term reflects the fact that everybody fails, and some more publicly than others. Yet when you fail in aspects of your career as in other areas, you always have a choice—to give up then and there, or to get up and keep going. Imagine if U.S. Supreme Court Justice Ruth Bader Ginsberg let failure stop her. Only the second woman ever appointed to the Supreme Court, Ginsberg faced—and ultimately overcame—unimaginable odds and obstacles throughout her rise to her present position. Despite graduating first in her class from Columbia University Law School, Ginsberg was reportedly turned down by 14 law firms where she applied for a job since they refused to hire a woman.[1]

Even J.K. Rowling, author of the wildly successful Harry Potter series, started out her writing career the same way that many writers do—with a stack of rejection letters—before finding a publisher who believed in her book. Rowling credits her initial failure with helping her to strip away "the inessential"—and forcing her to keep putting her energy into what mattered to her most.[2]

What if Ginsberg and Rowling had let their significant setbacks—which some would have interpreted as failures—discourage them and stop them in their tracks? What if instead of pursuing their dreams, they had decided that it wasn't worth the risk? The world would never have received the benefits of their unique gifts and contributions.

The fact is that while those with very public roles and performances often have visible failures that are broadcast widely, many people suffer setbacks privately. In her article "A CV of Failures,"[3] Melanie Stephan makes the point that scientists (and we can substitute people in every industry) often carefully develop untrue success narratives that minimize or hide their setbacks. To counteract this tendency to keep professional failures a secret, **Stephan** publicized the programs she didn't get into, the papers that journals rejected, and the fellowships that went to someone else. By being candid about her own failures, she hoped to shine a light on how frequently failure precedes success, noting that people who apply for an academic fellowship have only a 15 percent chance of being accepted, on average.[4]

While it may feel temporarily safer to conceal your professional stumbles, this decision can convince other professionals—falsely—that they are the only ones whose careers are not on a constant upward trajectory. Likewise, when others hide their failures from you, this seeming yet untrue perfection can result in feeling very alone when you experience a failure.

Keeping a list of your setbacks alongside your successes can help you maintain perspective on what it takes to achieve success. Sharing such a list with your professional networks also might help you and others rebound faster from rejection when it happens. To get used to what it feels like to communicate more honestly about your failures, try the exercise below.

EXERCISE A: WRITE A FAILURE LETTER

Research has shown that writing about a traumatic event helps people find meaning in their distress and feel more determined to move forward.[5] The writing process makes the emotional reaction to a major setback more manageable and helps curtail rumination about the details of what happened. While your professional situation might not qualify as a full-fledged trauma, you still might benefit from taking a similar approach. Try crafting a Failure Letter as follows:

For three days in a row, write about a failure that you experienced in your professional career. Choose something that deeply affected you; it can be an event that happened recently or a past event that still bothers you. Each session when you sit down to write, take the time to explore your deepest emotions and thoughts about the situation. You can write about the same issue each day, or about several different experiences.

Don't worry about spelling, sentence structure, or grammar—just write down what comes to you about each circumstance. When should you write? Journaling can be very effective if you write whenever you notice that you are thinking or worrying about something too much. Set a length of time that you feel comfortable with—10 to 20 minutes is a good benchmark, but feel free to write for longer or shorter periods as needed. Continue putting your thoughts on the page until the time you've decided upon is up, and try not to censor your emotions.

If it feels difficult to write about these experiences, here are some suggestions on how to keep your thoughts flowing:

- Remind yourself that you need not share your writing with anyone. You can always throw away your notes (or delete the computer file) when you complete the exercise.

- Because you're writing about challenging emotions, it might help to take a break from your writing.

- Remind yourself that by going through the journaling process, you'll be helping to process your feelings about what happened and gain clarity on the incidents of failure.

ACCEPT FAILURE FOR WHAT IT IS

Who doesn't love the feeling of winning, of being proven right and being outwardly successful? Who doesn't love the "high" that you get from others' validation of your talents and skills? Failing, on the other hand, is painful. There is no point in sugar coating it—it feels awful. When my client Justin was laid off for the first time after an illustrious 25-year career where he'd reached the level of vice president, he was devastated. He had never experienced a large-scale professional disappointment like this before, and it hit him hard.

As Justin's career coach, my ultimate goal was to help him brainstorm ways to find new employment. But when Justin and I met for the first time soon after his layoff, his anger was palpable: "Don't push me in a direction I don't want to go," he warned. "I'm leaving the field that I'm in." Clearly, before I could help Justin effectively determine his next career steps, he first needed to move through his grief about the situation.

When you experience what you interpret as a failure, it can shatter your self-esteem and send you into an emotional nosedive. No matter how confident you may have felt before the incident, you might immediately start questioning your capabilities, career direction, and in the short-term, almost everything. That's why the first thing to do after you've experienced a significant career setback is to allow yourself to feel angry, sad, and disappointed. It's important to go through this process before you try to problem-solve—and before deciding what you want to do next. You won't likely make good choices from a place of emotional pain.

EXERCISE B: ARE YOU GRIEVING A JOB LOSS?

As you saw from Justin's story, reactions to the loss of a job closely mirror the five stages of grief, which include denial that something bad has happened, anger about the situation, bargaining to try to get back to status quo, depression that you can't change the circumstances, and finally, acceptance of your new reality. In the early days after being laid off or fired, it can be very difficult to problem-solve when you're knee-deep in denial, hurt, and anger. The following exercise will help you understand which stage of the grief process you're experiencing with your job loss while offering suggestions for moving more gracefully through these phases. Begin by answering these questions:

1. How long has it been since you lost or left your job?
    a. 1 month or less
    b. 3 to 6 months
    c. 6 months to 1 year
    d. 1 year or more

2. Choose the answer that best describes your feelings about the following statement: When I think about losing my job I…
    a. Still can't believe it.
    b. Am furious and believe the outcome could have been different.
    c. Fantasize about ways I can convince my boss to change his or her mind.
    d. Feel depressed and somewhat hopeless.
    e. Accept the decision even though I don't like it.

3. Choose the answer that best describes your current state:
   a. I have trouble focusing and find my mind replaying what happened repeatedly.
   b. Although I have moments of feeling low, I'm more optimistic about the future and am moving forward in my job search.
   c. The past is the past—instead of spending energy trying to rewrite it, I'm looking forward to creating a new future.

4. Choose the answer that best reflects your feeling about the future:
   a. I'm not optimistic about my prospects for finding a new job. Who wants to hire someone who has been laid off?
   b. I have marketable skills and the determination to move ahead.
   c. Parting ways with my last employer was a blessing in disguise.

If it has been less than three months since your last day of employment, you may still be experiencing the early stages of grief and not feel ready to move on yet. If this is the case, reach out to supportive family and friends, or seek out a therapist or career coach to help you during this transition. If you answered "a," "b," "c," or "d" to question 2, you are still grieving your loss. Be kind to yourself during this period and get the support you need. The same advice holds true if you answered "a" to questions 3 and 4. If you selected "e" for question 2 and "b" or "c" for questions 3 and 4, you are moving past your grief to acceptance.

GET GRITTY

What can we learn from Justice Ginsberg and others who have had painful—and sometimes very public—failures yet also enormous successes? In a nutshell, these heroes are excellent role models for perseverance and tenacity in the face of what feels at the moment like permanent defeat. Let's return again to *Harry Potter*, since the protagonist of the seven-novel fantasy series has as much to teach us about responding to failure as the author does. How many times throughout the series did the orphan Harry Potter escape death before finally being able to kill Lord Voldemort during the Battle of Hogwarts? How many Death Eaters, beasts, and spells did Harry survive in the most frightening of circumstances before achieving his goals at long last?

One quality that helps people persist despite failure and fear is grit, which relates to your determination, strength of character, courage, and resolve to move forward—no matter what—to ultimately reach your goals. Grit gives you the strength to cope with bad days, as well as with trauma or crisis. Along with Harry Potter, my client Justin is another good example of this type of tenacity in the face of apparent failure. He did not end up quitting his field after all. After grieving the loss of his job, Justin got gritty. He set up 50 networking meetings with former colleagues. His network validated that Justin's job loss was not a measure of his value, but was instead a temporary setback from which he could rise and prosper. These discussions with professional peers also helped Justin regain his sense of self-worth. In the eight years since, he has experienced many career successes and continues to work toward his overriding career goals in his original field.

Angela Duckworth's psychological research has found that grit is one of the best predictors of exceptional performance, both at work and in classrooms. Specifically, she and her research team examined why some people accomplish more than others when talent and intelligence/IQ are equal. The answer, they found, was due to how much persistence the individuals exhibited.[6]

What can we learn from this research? One key point is that gritty people don't seek perfection every step along the way, but strive for an overall experience of excellence instead—which can be punctuated by failures. While the terms "perfection" and "excellence" may sound similar, this distinction is significant. As discussed earlier, perfectionism may cause you to give up prematurely or avoid trying things outside of your comfort zone for fear of failing. But in this scenario, perfectionists are chasing *someone else's* perception of an ideal, which is like pursuing a mirage: it's always out there yet never attainable.

Excellence, on the other hand, allows for missteps en route to your destination—as long as you keep getting back on track toward *your own* vision. The ancient Greeks called excellence Arête, which they also associated with meaning and purpose. Arête in Greek mythology was a goddess of virtue, so its definition has also come to mean living up to one's full potential. By getting back on the horse and not giving up on his career goals, my client Justin used his grit to demonstrate a commitment to excellence in the face of what initially felt like career-ending failure. As a result of his persistence, he moved beyond the rough patch to reach his career potential.

HAVE YOU FAILED OR DID YOU QUIT?

If Supreme Court Justice Ruth Ginsberg had given up on her dreams to be a lawyer when one of the law firms she initially wanted to join didn't hire her, would you consider her a failure, or would you think she quit prematurely? The successful results of her persistence suggest that the latter would have been the case—it wasn't her failure not to get asked on board, but if she had not pushed forward toward her larger goals, then she would have given up too soon to enjoy the success in her field that she eventually achieved.

Our culture rewards instant results—the number of "Likes" you receive on Facebook, the number of people who view your LinkedIn profile, how many visitors frequent your blog. It's no wonder that so many of us seek feel-good instant outcomes. How often have you expected something to materialize immediately, and when you didn't get it in the first 30, 60, or 90 days, you assumed that you'd failed and decided to move on?

The problem with this type of reaction to things taking more time to unfold is that it's difficult to ever know whether you've failed or quit too soon. That's why it's important that in spite of experiencing setbacks, you avoid declaring failure at the first obstacle—or sometimes even the second or third—and instead learn to pivot, iterate, and persist. How do you know if you've failed? If you can think of alternative routes to reach your goal, then it probably isn't a failure. You may just need to apply some grit.

American culture, of course, isn't the only one that values persistence. Finnish culture has it's own word for persistence—sisu. Translated as "Finnish spirit," sisu is less about achievement than about bravely facing challenges with determination.[7] Again, no matter which culture, it's about the mindset that enables individuals to "power on" even after they feel like they've reached the end of their mental or physical resources.

TREAT FAILURE LIKE THE BUDDHA

According to Buddhist teaching, what causes us misery in our lives is trying to avoid pain and seek happiness—the belief that we could experience lasting security and happiness if only we never screwed up and could always do the right thing. Pema Chödrön explains in her book *Fail, Fail Again, Fail Better*[8] how when people fail, the common tendency is to blame someone else or blame themselves. It's human nature to suddenly jump to thinking that we—or somebody—screwed something up. But why is this our kneejerk reaction?

Chödrön makes the point that intellectually, we know that seeking certainty is a losing battle, but emotionally that's what we keep attempting. As long as we run from discomfort, the cycle of unhappiness and disappointment continues. Accepting the feelings of pain and disappointment helps us to develop inner strength and resilience.

In fact, as Buddhists know, suffering has much to teach us. If you use the opportunity when it arises in your career, feeling bad can motivate you to look for answers, and can lead you toward new destinations you might not have thought about before. So try to be more Zen about failure. The reality is that you can prepare well, but you can't ever predict the twists and turns that life will take. You need to be prepared for the rug to be pulled out from under you once in a while, and then be just as prepared to get right back up.

TRY THIS

When you experience a failure, do you punish yourself? If your tendency is to cancel your gym membership or massage appointment as a reaction to a disappointment, denying what you need won't solve your challenges and may make your disillusioned feelings even worse. Spend some time thinking about how you generally respond to failure. If you're used to punishing yourself, try a new, more positive approach to disappointment and do something nice for yourself! Brainstorm some of your favorite things that you can do to give yourself a treat, and return to this list when something goes wrong:

_____

_____

_____

As you incorporate the learnings of this chapter, remember that when a scientist runs an experiment, there are all sorts of potential outcomes—

some positive and some negative. Regardless of whether an outcome is good or bad, though, every outcome leads to new data points that wouldn't have been gained without the experience that feels like failure.

With this perspective in mind, recognize that your failures are simply data points that can help lead you to a better outcome in the future. Return to these strategies for investigating your failures as needed, to help you excavate how this information can inform your future ventures. Let's bring it all home now—in the final chapter, you'll see how you can reach your career goals and stick with them for the long haul simply by changing your thinking patterns and behaviors.

ELEVEN

Making It Happen and Sticking With It

Throughout this book, you've learned about letting go of what's holding you back to thrive in your career, using research-based strategies to quiet your inner critic and uncover self-sabotaging thoughts and behaviors. You've also practiced how to get in touch with your deepest career desires, strengths, and values. Now it's time to put these collective concepts into action and start making your career vision come to life!

When people contact me from the brink of a career transition, they often express something similar to what my client Amit did, when he admitted: "I want to change careers, but I feel stuck. I'm very unhappy where I am, but I'm not sure what my best options are, and working full time leaves me very little time to look for a new job."

Like Amit, people often hope that the job of their dreams will magically appear, forgetting that discovering a satisfying new career is a process of taking small steps that ultimately lead to arriving at your destination. Even if you are very busy, there are little things you can do to begin moving in the direction of your goals. But it takes a double dose of tenacity first to make it happen, and then to stick with it for the long haul. And before you can start moving toward your goals, you need to understand how to effectively set them.

GOALS VS. STRATEGIC SYSTEMS

The reason Amit felt overwhelmed by the prospect of changing jobs is that he didn't know what specific steps would help him get where he wanted to go. In other words, he needed help with goal setting. A goal is a desired end state that provides a focus for your motivational energy. Yet when it comes to goal setting and attainment, there's an important distinction to understand between your actual goals, and the strategic systems or processes you plan to use to reach those end points. Your goals are what you're aiming for, but it's the systems you put in place—and how efficiently you use them—that determine your progress.

Understanding and applying this distinction between what you want and how you plan to get it is crucial to realizing your goals. Here are a few examples of different types of strategic systems that might correspond to particular goals:

- If you're in career transition, your *goal* might be to find a new job. Your *strategic system* might include writing a resume, updating your LinkedIn profile, and identifying your network.

- If you're starting a consulting business, your *goal* might be to make $100K+ in the first year. Your *strategic system* might include identifying your buyers, creating your branding materials, and developing a selling process.

- If you're a writer, your *goal* might be to write a book. Your *strategic system* might be developing a regular writing schedule that you follow each week.

- Keep in mind that starting small with short-term achievable goals can help build up your confidence as you move forward toward larger goals. Baby steps are also important because while dreaming about goals in the distant future can be fun, it's human nature to prefer a payoff in the short-term to keep you motivated. Goals that are planned for the near future generate more psychic attention than goals that are further off. The more imminent the goal, the bigger the influence on your behavior. So, if you feel stymied like Amit did about how to move forward in a new career direction, be sure to start by figuring out what your strategic system is as well as your specific goals, so that you know what you want and exactly how to get there, small step by small step.

TRY THIS

To help you get the hang of working with a strategic system to reach your goals, identify one career goal that you'd like to achieve in the next six months to a year. Remember to make it challenging, but also realistic. In other words, be sure that with focused effort, your goal is achievable in the timeframe you've chosen. Write your goal below.

My career goal is to: _____

Next, outline the strategic systems you plan to use to achieve your goal. List them as actions in the logical order you will follow to reach goal completion. As in the examples above, your path to reach your goal should be built on small but deliberate steps that are identifiable and trackable. List yours below, along with the dates you expect to complete each action item.

As my strategic system to reach the goal stated above, the actions I plan to take and my timeline include:

Action	Completion Date
1.	
2.	
3.	
4.	
5.	
6.	

Continue until you've listed all the actions you'll need to reach your milestone. If it helps you to figure out what steps are needed, work backward from your goal, listing actions from last to first instead of first to last. The actions you've listed are in effect your strategic process that can help you successfully accomplish your goal.

THE POWER OF HOPEFULNESS

Your attitude also plays an important role in reaching and sticking with your goals. If you're dragging your feet about making a change or feeling hopeless about improving your circumstances, it can affect your success, particularly during career transitions. Likewise, cultivating a feeling of hope can help you reach your goals more quickly.

Why is maintaining hopefulness so important? Imagine a Caribbean vacation or European cruise you've been dreaming about. Just thinking about going on your adventure makes you feel excited and propels you forward to take care of all the logistics, from getting your passport in order to buying your tickets and braving the trains, planes, and automobiles necessary to reach your destination. The same type of energy applies to feeling hopeful about your career next steps. Consider the excitement you feel when you anticipate the new consulting company you hope to launch, or leaving a job that's a poor fit for one that you're passionate about.

Humans have the unique distinction of being able to imagine the future. We can think about upcoming events in ways that no other animal can. This ability is what allows us to hope. Derived from Old English, the word "hope" means to "leap forward with expectation." Hope plays such an important role in our lives that scientists have studied its role in helping us achieve our goals.

One part of hope is approaching your goals with enough energy and determination to see them through—in other words, willpower. Every day, in one form or another, you use your willpower. You resist the urge to check Facebook instead of finishing your expense report. You bite your tongue when you'd like to respond to a colleague's unpleasant comment. While it makes you feel good to use your willpower for reasons like this throughout the day, a growing body of research shows that your willpower is not unlimited. Some experts liken willpower to a muscle that can get fatigued from overuse and needs to be replenished.

Some of the earliest evidence of this effect came from the lab of Roy Baumeister. In one study,[1] he brought subjects into a room filled with the smell of freshly baked cookies. The table before them held a plate of the cookies and a bowl of radishes. Some subjects were asked to sample the cookies, while others were asked to eat the radishes. Afterward, they were given 30 minutes to complete a difficult geometric puzzle. Baumeister and his colleagues found that people who ate radishes (and resisted the enticing cookies) gave up on the puzzle after about 8 minutes, while the lucky cookie-eaters persevered for nearly 19 minutes, on average. Drawing on willpower to resist the cookies, it seemed, drained the subjects' self-control for subsequent situations.

You're probably quite familiar with goal thinking and using willpower to try to achieve it: I want to write a book, get a promotion, or find better work-life balance. It's often tougher to figure out the *specific steps* necessary to achieve a goal—the strategic system mentioned above. Yet this type of planning is essential, particularly in the case of long-term goals, because these are the actions that help you get from point A to point B to point C. What's more, when you focus your energy on the strategic planning part of the picture, you don't have to worry about lessened self-control over time the way you do with goals that involve willpower. Unlike willpower, working on your strategic systems does not draw on limited resources, so it makes sense to shift gears as needed for goal achievement.

Where does hope enter into all of this? Research[2] has shown that when hopeful people encounter an obstacle, they try to think of ways around it. Because some of those plans may not succeed, hopeful people generate many plans—different possible strategic systems—in order to circumvent possible obstacles. When people who are low in hope experience a challenge, they often get stuck and frustrated after failing at a single solution, and their performance or mood can suffer. Hopeful people, on the other hand, deal much more gracefully with everyday obstacles and may even become energized when they hit a sticky patch, knowing they'll find ways to get unstuck. People with low hope stay stuck.

Another component of future-oriented thinking that psychologists have studied is called agency thinking. Agency is the beliefs individuals hold regarding their ability to initiate and continue moving on pathways toward reaching their goals. It is by marshaling agency thinking— another part of hopefulness—that you become motivated to initiate and sustain the deliberate steps toward your desired ends.

Gene comes to mind as someone who scores high on the hope scale. A former CEO, Gene found himself at a crossroads when his company was acquired and his position eliminated. After applying for various C-level positions, he found himself growing increasingly uncomfortable continuing in the direction that he'd been heading. Realizing that he no longer wanted to work 80-100 hours a week and guessing that his 55+ age might increasingly work against him, he wanted to find a new path to employment.

Although initially frustrated when he didn't gain traction on the CEO/COO path, Gene quickly pivoted to generate different options. He began by creating a list of alternative ideas including sales or sales management positions, teaching at the college level, transitioning to the nonprofit sector, or going into business for himself. His "workaround" strategy is an example of thinking about strategic systems rather than goals alone: "If I can't get employment by pursuing option A, I'll figure out three or four alternatives." Gene ultimately chose the entrepreneurial path when he realized that specific skills and knowledge he developed early in his career could be put to use in developing a franchise. Agency thinking also helped him through the tough times, because he believed in his ability to generate alternatives and move forward feeling hopeful. He continuously researched and learned about his new career options, and felt excited to share the insights he had gleaned. Gene's hopeful approach served him well in allowing him to reach his goals.

To explore the flip side of hope, consider another client I worked with named Carl, who was a marketing executive. While interested in a career change, Carl found it challenging to explore options outside of his specialized area of expertise. Not being able to generate pathways to more than one option left him feeling hopeless, and weakened his agency thinking. As Carl's coach, I could see that he had lost faith in his ability to make a change and needed a boost to help him regain a sense of control. If you feel that way about your career options, the ideas in the exercise below are designed to help you strengthen your agency thinking.

EXERCISE A: HOW TO HARNESS HOPE

You can have clear and measurable goals yet still feel stuck. Here are some suggestions on how to cultivate a hopeful mindset to get unstuck:

To increase energy toward your goals:

1. **Ask "why not."** Try to imagine some potential career goals that seem out of reach and instead of second-guessing your ability to get there, ask "why not?" This can be freeing when contemplating new goals.

2. **Get crazy.** Begin by saying "There's no way I could…" From this launching pad, write down some goals that seem totally unreachable. You'll probably laugh at your outrageous ideas, but it's a great way to boost your hopefulness.

3. **Create stepping stone goals.** Identify short-term steps that will help you reach your ultimate goal. For job seekers, these steps might include identifying your accomplishments, creating a resume, and setting up informational interviews to get information or advice.

4. **Focus on the present.** Think about what you are learning and enjoying while working toward your goal. This will help you notice the progress you are making and stay aware of the journey as well as the destination.

To increase awareness of alternative routes toward reaching your goal:

1. **Set specific intentions.** Two of the most common reasons for not achieving goals are difficulty getting started, and sticking to long-term goals because of distractions, temptations, or competing goals. Research has shown that setting specific intentions in relation to your strategic systems increases your chance of following through successfully and can help you move toward your goals.[3] For example, let's say your goal is to create a new resume. Working and parenting leave you little time, so you've procrastinated on updating your branding because of the commitment. Setting an intention about your strategy can help you break the larger task into several more manageable tasks. The first part of the equation is determining what time of day and where you plan to work on it. Will you get up 30 minutes earlier and devote that time to your resume, or will you devote an hour or two on a Saturday or Sunday? Where will you work on it—your kitchen table or Starbucks? The second component outlines the steps you will take to get there, such as looking over past performance reviews and recording your accomplishments.

2. **Create a mental dress rehearsal.** Imagine each step required to achieve your "sub-goals"—steps along the way to reaching your ultimate goal—as specifically as possible. What will you do and say? For example, if your goal is to ask for a promotion, imagine yourself setting up an appointment with your boss, making small talk at the beginning of the meeting, telling her how much you enjoy working for the company, and detailing your contributions over the last year. Imagine that your boss is smiling, and then envision yourself confidently asking her for the promotion as you describe your achievements.

3.   **Design an alternate roadmap.** The original path that you set toward a goal may need to be modified along the way, so it's important to be flexible in your response. As you move forward, you may realize that the plan you at first identified may conflict with other priorities, causing you to spread yourself too thin from trying to accomplish too much at once. If, for example, you decided to get up at 5:30 every morning to write a blog, you might find yourself exhausted by the end of the first week. If that happened, you could apply the learning toward redirecting your plan: in this case, it might be better to set a goal of getting up early three days a week instead of every day to avoid burnout. It's also worth reevaluating your plan when an unexpected opportunity presents itself, such as when your boss asks you to take on an exciting over-seas assignment. You can only accomplish meaningful goals when you're willing to question assumptions regularly and pivot as needed.

To increase belief in yourself:

1.   **Recall your earlier successes.** Remind yourself of situations when you overcame a big challenge. What strengths did you use to find a viable workaround? How did you feel when you achieved your goal?

2.   **Learn to laugh at yourself.** What humor can you find in the often absurdity of difficulty? Think of a tough situation that you weathered at work, and see if you can find something funny about it.

3.   **Redefine or find a substitute goal.** Midcourse corrections are frequently needed as part of successful goal achievement. For example, if my client Gene, whose story I described earlier, had stuck to his original goal of landing a new CEO or COO

role, he would not have been true to his ultimate values and authenticity. Gene also realized after considering alternate goals that there was a faster and more enjoyable path to employment. This meant letting go of his original goal and revisiting his options. Is there a goal that you need to let go of today so that you can do something even better?

THE KITE AND STRING PRINCIPLE OF GOAL SETTING

If you've ever flown a kite, then you understand how integral the tautness of string is to getting the kite to fly. Leave the string too loose, and you won't get your kite in the air. Pull it too tight, and you'll bring the kite crashing down. The tension has to be just right on the string to create the perfect resistance needed to lift the kite and make it soar. This analogy mirrors the case for goal setting. If you set a goal that lacks challenge, then you'll likely lose interest and become bored. But if you set a goal that is essentially unachievable, you will soon lack the motivation for reaching it.

The goal you choose has to be attainable, but challenging enough to keep you interested in pursuing it. "Stretch goals" are motivating because they require more effort to attain and be satisfied with than do easy-to-reach objectives. Your feelings of success at work will increase when you are able to grow by pursuing and attaining goals that are challenging, relevant, and meaningful.

One of the reasons I decided to write this book was to challenge myself to see if I could achieve an audacious goal. Challenging myself wasn't the only reason, of course. Sharing my passion for finding work satisfaction is what drives me. Nevertheless, I could have chosen a goal that was far less bold. Having functioned in my comfort zone for a long time, I understood what researchers have long known about goal setting: as shown in a study of people in managerial and professional jobs in

Germany, those who set goals that they perceive as difficult yet attainable feel a greater sense of well-being and success.[4] Interestingly, this same study showed that even those who lacked goal attainment in their personal life experienced greater well-being when they experienced goal progress on the job, indicating that success in one realm can compensate for failure in another.

Recall for a moment the concept of flow described in Chapter 8. Clear goals and a balance between high challenge and high skill are two conditions that are helpful to entering a flow state. And it's in a flow state that you can experience the intense concentration required to reach your goals. Not sure whether or not your goal-setting technique is serving you as well as it could? Try the next exercise.

EXERCISE B: IS YOUR GOAL SETTING WORKING FOR YOU OR AGAINST YOU?

To evaluate your goal-setting process, read the following questions and then answer by choosing one of the options.

1. I set lots of goals in the hope that I will achieve a few of them.
   a. Frequently
   b. Occasionally
   c. Rarely

2. I have difficulty achieving my goals.
   a. Frequently
   b. Occasionally
   c. Rarely

3. If I'm struggling to meet a goal, I set sub-goals to find quick wins.
   a. Frequently
   b. Occasionally
   c. Rarely

4. I tie my work-related objectives to personal values.
   a. Frequently
   b. Occasionally
   c. Rarely

5. I set low standards so that my goals are easy to meet.
   a. Frequently
   b. Occasionally
   c. Rarely

6. I don't ask for support from friends and colleagues if I become unmotivated about a goal.
   a. Frequently
   b. Occasionally
   c. Rarely

7. I regularly monitor how I am doing, so that I can measure how well I'm progressing toward my goals.
   a. Frequently
   b. Occasionally
   c. Rarely

8. My personal values are relevant to my work-related objectives.
   a. Frequently
   b. Occasionally
   c. Rarely

9. I don't set an end date for achieving my goals, so I won't feel bad if I don't reach them.
    a. Frequently
    b. Occasionally
    c. Rarely

10. I seek out resources that help me reach my goals.
    a. Frequently
    b. Occasionally
    c. Rarely

11. Before making new plans, I reflect on my existing commitments to make sure that I don't take on too much.
    a. Frequently
    b. Occasionally
    c. Rarely

12. If I fail to meet a target, I move on without reflecting on what went wrong.
    a. Frequently
    b. Occasionally
    c. Rarely

If you responded "Rarely" to all or most of questions 1, 2, 5, 6, 9, and 12 and "Frequently" to all or most of questions 3, 7, 8, 10, and 11, then you are well on your way to setting goals that are personally meaningful and that ensure you have the time and resources to achieve them.

If your answers are mostly in reverse—i.e., you answered "Frequently" to all or most of questions 1, 2, 5, 6, 9, and 12 and "Rarely" to all or most of 3, 7, 8, 10, and 11—then you may be setting goals that aren't motivating enough for you, or may be overly focused on what others expect of you rather than what you want for yourself. If that's the case, then go back and revisit Exercise A to review the strategies for harnessing the power of hope more effectively. And read on to learn more about smarter goal setting.

MAKE YOUR GOALS SMARTER

When clients like Amit described at the start of this chapter contact me because of their inability to reach their goal of a successful career transition, it's generally because they haven't mapped out their goals and strategic systems clearly enough. But building in measurable checkpoints to ensure that you receive feedback along the way can also help.

Research in **goal setting** and motivation shows that setting clear goals and receiving input on progress motivates employees.[5] It's not just the achievement of the long-term goal—in Amit's case, finding a new job—that's rewarding. Working toward a goal is also a primary source of motivation, which in turn provides the internal incentive to keep going.

In order to achieve progress, your goal needs to be both specific and measurable. For career changers, measurable interim objectives might include:

- Developing a job objective (industry, title, function, responsibilities)
- Creating a resume or LinkedIn profile
- Crafting an elevator pitch
- Identifying and prioritizing networking contacts
- Building and implementing a personal marketing plan

Is your ultimate goal really attainable? While it's nice to dream and be confident, some goals are just not realistic based on the actual circumstances. Just as it would be impossible for me to win a tennis match against Serena Williams since I can barely serve the ball over the net, it's highly unlikely that a marketing executive can become an astronaut late in his or her career. Unless the marketing exec is willing and can afford to go back to school to earn a degree in aeronautical engineering and devote many years to rebuilding an entire career in the new direction, rocketing to outer space is not going to happen in this lifetime.

For this reason, be sure that your long-term aim is in the realm of reality, not fantasy. A way to test the viability of your goal is to outline all of the steps needed to attain it, as well as obstacles that will likely arise. The exercise below will help you test your assumptions by designing a goal-setting plan in a unique way.

EXERCISE C: PLAN BACKWARD

Unlike traditional planning that requires developing a set of steps from beginning to end, backward planning is designed to help you gain a different perspective and, perhaps, identify different milestones as a result.

Here's how it works:

Step 1: Write down your eventual goal. What specifically do you want to achieve, and by what date?

Example: "By December 31, I plan to be the marketing director for a start-up technology company."

Step 2: Ask yourself what milestones you need to accomplish in order to achieve your ultimate goal. What do you have to do—and by when—to ensure that you'll be in a position to reach your final objective?

Example: "I will identify a mentor in the industry who will help make introductions and validate that my personal branding will resonate with high-tech CEOs by September 1."

Step 3: Work backward some more. What do you need to complete before that second-to-last goal?

Example: "By June 1, I will create a resume that outlines my successes as a marketing manager, and I'll complete a course in social media marketing."

Step 4: Work back again. What do you need to do to make sure the previous goal is reached?

Example: "I will speak on an industry panel talking about trends in high-tech marketing by March 1."

Step 5: Continue to work back, in the same way, until you identify the very first, most preliminary milestone that you need to accomplish en route to your goal.

Planning backward is a great addition to the traditional planning process, and it gives you a much fuller appreciation of what it may take to achieve success. After all, the more alternatives you have, the better your final plan will likely be. The strategy of thinking from the end zone forces you to brainstorm from a completely new perspective, decreasing the chances of overlooking steps you might otherwise miss if you only use a forward-looking plan.

PRETEND IT'S NEW YEAR'S EVE

What is it about the arrival of a new year that causes us to make resolutions? About 40-50 percent of Americans reportedly make a New Year's resolution.[6] Is there more to it than guilt about overeating during the holidays and the obligatory goal to lose weight? It turns out that setting virtuous goals at the beginning of the year can be very effective because of something known as "temporal landmarks."[7] Temporal landmarks create what researchers have dubbed a "fresh start effect," helping us mentally distinguish between our current situation and our desired future.[8] In other words, when you feel that your past failures are behind you and the slate is wiped clean, you can turn your attention toward achieving future success, making you feel more motivated and inspired to work hard to reach your goals.

The good news is that New Year's is only one of many temporal landmarks you can choose to kickstart your goal setting. For example, the beginning of a month, a birthday, a holiday, the first day of spring, daylight savings time, or baseball opening day in your hometown can be equally motivating if you use these as temporal landmarks.

TRY THIS

Ready to choose your fresh start? In the next week to 10 days, pick a goal you want to achieve, and the temporal landmark when you plan to start. Keep track of your progress. If you find your resolve drifting, pick a new fresh start date in the not too distant future to keep you motivated.

ANTICIPATE OBSTACLES

What else can help you reach your goals? You may be wondering if positive thinking might play a role in goal attainment. But research shows that positive thinking will only get you so far when it comes to following through on your goals.[9] Plus as you've learned, your willpower is in limited supply, so relying too heavily on it without using other strategies may leave you disappointed.

What can you use as an alternative to overreliance on positive thinking and willpower? Psychologists have found that anticipating obstacles that may stand in the way of your goals enables you to achieve more than ignoring or minimizing their existence.[10] In fact, research shows that only when people combine positive thinking with a clear view of potential obstacles will they achieve their desired results.[11] Wishful thinking may make you feel good in the short-term, but you're less likely to buck up and make the strong, persistent effort that is needed to realize challenging but feasible wishes. What does help with goal attainment is mental contrasting,[12] a strategy that combines positive fantasy about the future with a visualization of the obstacles standing in the way. Even more beneficial is setting specific intentions, which as discussed earlier allows you to address obstacles when they arise.

IT'S A CINCH BY THE INCH

Wherever you decide to start on your journey to authenticity and finding your path to greater career satisfaction, remember this: change takes time. Regardless of the behavior you're trying to change—whether it's not reading emails at night, letting go of your inner critic, or setting a goal of leaving your current job—ingrained patterns will threaten to pull you off course. That's the way the brain works, for better or for worse. While you may wish it were otherwise, if you pick too many things to work on at once, you will likely be setting yourself up for failure. Instead, to start, select one or two goals that are the most important to you, and be patient with yourself.

Habits take time to form. That's because whenever you change a behavioral pattern, your brain is working overtime to get used to the new one. In a study[13] published in the *European Journal of Social Psychology*, a research team decided to figure out just how long it actually takes to form a habit. The study examined the habits of 96 people over a 12-week period. All participants chose one new habit for the 12 weeks and reported each day on whether or not they did the behavior and how automatic the behavior felt.

Some people chose simple activities like "drinking a bottle of water with lunch." Others chose more difficult tasks like "running for 15 minutes before dinner." At the end of the 12 weeks, the researchers looked at how long it took each person to go from starting a new behavior to automatically doing it. On average, they found that it takes more than two months before a new behavior becomes automatic. How long it takes a new habit to form can vary widely depending on the behavior, the person, and the circumstances. In the study, it took anywhere from 18 days to 254 days for people to form a new habit.

Remember, your goal is not to be perfect; it's to be excellent. Striving for excellence means remaining true to your values, interests, passions, and priorities so that you can craft a career that is aligned with your authentic self. If you're not used to living this way, this change will take time. Most importantly, it will require patience with yourself when you fall back into old patterns, make mistakes, and don't progress as quickly as you had imagined you would.

If you find yourself falling back on ingrained perfectionistic patterns instead of developing new habits, think of the following:

- **Know.** Get to know your inner critic by becoming more aware of your self-defeating patterns of thinking and behavior. What are your triggers?

- **Challenge.** Challenge your automatic patterns of thinking and question your beliefs. Is it so important that you read emails at 10 PM? What would happen if you didn't? Do you know anyone with uneven books on their shelves? Do you think any less of them because their books aren't perfectly aligned? What are the costs and benefits of spending time making everything "just so"?

- **Change.** Change your behavior by taking calculated risks and stepping outside your comfort zone. Practice making mistakes that are reasonable. Say no to taking on an extra project when you're swamped instead of saying yes—as you would usually do to please the other person—and overwhelming yourself as a result.

GOING FORWARD

Throughout this book, you've gained an insider's view on current research into why and how you can thrive in your career—in spite of your inner critic and any setbacks or failures that you may have experienced. Now you can see that possibilities exist within you to reach higher and do more than you ever thought possible.

Too often in the past, you may have settled for the status quo even if it didn't meet your needs, simply because you didn't believe that you deserved or could achieve more. But now you've seen validated by science that happiness is not about how much money you make or the status you achieve. Life satisfaction comes from living in accordance with your own values and interests, not from striving for perfection as your inner critic—or any outer ones—might have you believe.

In conjunction with the research on well-being, you now have practical tools to help you challenge false assumptions, grow beyond common personal and professional setbacks, and move ahead in your career. As you continue on your path—this time without your self-critical mindset in tow—I hope you'll return to the exercises in this book again and again. Use them whenever you need them to take control of your career in new and wonderful ways that you never imagined, and to become more resilient, gritty, and hopeful.

Acknowledgements

I have been very fortunate to have people in my life to support me when I needed to move forward with a difficult decision. Choosing to write a book was one of those instances. More time consuming than I imagined possible, discipline alone is not enough to persist for the hours, days and months needed to persevere. Without the support of a number of special individuals, this book might never have been written.

Special gratitude goes to Robin Madell, the editor of this book. More than an editor, Robin was a close collaborator. She smoothed the rough edges of my writing, bridged the transitions with clarity and challenged the hundreds of times I wanted to change the title. As a journalist and a career writer in her own right, she believed in the concept of this book from the get-go, and never flagged in her enthusiasm and encouragement. Robin, I could never say thank you enough!

My thanks to the leaders of the Whole Being Institute, psychologist and author, Tal Ben Shahar, CEO, Megan McDonough, teachers, Maria Sirois and Megha-Nancy Buttenheim. Tal, if it were not for your foresight in bringing positive psychology research out of the ivy-covered halls of academia to create the Certificate in Positive Psychology, I would never have been exposed to your brilliant teaching and passion for making this research accessible. Megan, your leadership inspired me to reach high and boldly. For that I am very grateful. Maria, you made vulnerability and failure OK, enabling me to acknowledge the cost of staying in my comfort zone. Megha, you taught me the value of bridging body health and brain health through a love of movement in a way that only you can.

To my husband, Gareth and children Samantha and Harrison, your support was invaluable. For all the times you patiently understood when I said, "Can it wait? I have a chapter to finish." Thank you, thank you for your patience and support! These acknowledgements would not be complete without thanking my sweet dog, Jewel who sat by my side and snored comfortingly through my hours of writing without asking anything in return.

About the Author

Susan Peppercorn is a career management and personal branding coach who enables executives to go from surviving to thriving in their careers.

She is frequently quoted in top publications including the NY Times, Wall Street Journal, Fast Company, U.S. News and World Report and Business Insider. Her clients include individuals from Harvard University, Pfizer, Novartis, DigitasLBi, Forrester Research, and Blue Cross Blue Shield, to name a few.

Susan is a certified as a Positive Psychology Coach and was a teaching assistant for Tal Ben Shahar, who taught the most popular course at Harvard and started the certificate program in positive psychology. She is accredited by the International Coaching Federation (ICF), is an executive mentor for the Healthcare Businesswomen's Association (HBA) and a frequent speaker on topics related to career success and satisfaction.

Connect with Susan

www.positiveworkplacepartners.com
twitter.com/susanpeppercorn
linkedin.com/in/susanpeppercorn
facebook.com/positiveworkplace

Notes

Chapter 1
Getting to Know Your Inner Critic

1. "Number of Jobs Held in a Lifetime," National Longitudinal Surveys, U.S. Bureau of Labor Statistics, United States Department of Labor, April 19, 2016, https://www.bls.gov/nls/nlsfaqs.htm#anch41.

2. E. Tory Higgins. "Self-Discrepancy: A Theory Relating Self and Affect," *Psychological Review*, 94(3), 1987: 319-340, http://persweb.wabash.edu/facstaff/hortonr/articles%20for%20class/Higgins.pdf.

3. Nicole Kreisberg, *New Careers for Older Workers: Research Study*, American Institute for Economic Research, 2015, https://www.aier.org/sites/default/files/Files/Documents/Webform/AIER_OWS.pdf.

4. Carol Dweck, "Mindset for Achievement," Mindset, Mindsetonline.com, 2010, http://mindsetonline.com/howmindsetaffects/mindsetforachievement/index.html.

5.   "Carol Dweck Recommends the Best Books on Success," Five Books, Lifestyle, July 5, 2012, http://fivebooks.com/interview/carol-dweck-on-success/.

6.   Robert P. Gallagher, *National Survey of College Counseling Centers 2014*, American College Counseling Association (ACCA), The International Association of Counseling Services, Inc., Monograph Series Number 9V, 2014, http://0201.nccdn.net/1_2/000/000/088/0b2/NCCCS2014_v2.pdf.

7.   Sherrie Bourg Carter, "The Mind and Body Benefits of Optimism," *Psychology Today*, August 2012, https://www.psychologytoday.com/blog/high-octane-women/201208/the-mind-and-body-benefits-optimism-0.

8.   Heather Barry Kappes and Gabriele Oettingen, "Positive Fantasies About Idealized Futures Sap Energy," *Journal of Experimental Social Psychology*, (2011): 719–729, DOI: 10.1016/j.jesp.2011.02.003, http://www.psych.nyu.edu/oettingen/Barry%20Kappes,%20H.,%20&%20Oettingen,%20G.%20(2011).%20JESP.pdf.

Chapter 2
Career Myths and Confabulations:
What Happiness Isn't—And Is

1.   Sonja Lyubomirsky, *The Myths of Happiness: What Should Make You Happy, but Doesn't, What Shouldn't Make You Happy, but Does*, New York, NY: Penguin Group, 2013.

2.   Ed Diener, "Happiness: The Science of Subjective Well-Being," *Noba Textbook Series: Psychology*, Champaign, IL: DEF publishers,

2017, DOI:nobaproject.com, http://nobaproject.com/modules/happiness-the-science-of-subjective-well-being.

3. Belinda Luscombe, "Do We Need $75,000 a Year to Be Happy?" *Time Magazine*, September 6, 2010, http://content.time.com/time/magazine/article/0,9171,2019628,00.html.

4. D. Watson, L.A. Clark, and A. Tellegan, "Development and Validation of Brief Measures of Positive and Negative Affect: The PANAS Scales," *Journal of Personality and Social Psychology*, 54(6), 1988: 1063–1070, http://booksite.elsevier.com/9780123745170/Chapter%203/Chapter_3_Worksheet_3.1.pdf.

5. Ed Diener, Robert A. Emmons, Randy J. Larsen, and Sharon Griffin. "The Satisfaction With Life Scale," *Journal of Personality Assessment*, 49(1), 1985: 71-75, http://emmons.faculty.ucdavis.edu/wp-content/uploads/sites/90/2015/08/1985_5-SWLS.pdf.

6. University of Pennsylvania, "Positive Psychology Theory," Authentic Happiness, 2017, https://www.authentichappiness.sas.upenn.edu/learn.

7. Albert Bandura, "Self-efficacy: Toward a Unifying Theory of Behavior Change," *Psychological Review*, (84)2, 1977: 191-215, https://www.uky.edu/~eushe2/Bandura/Bandura1977PR.pdf.

8. Bettina S. Wiese and Alexandra M. Freund. "Goal Progress Makes One Happy, or Does It? Longitudinal Findings from the Work Domain," *Journal of Occupational and Organizational Psychology*, 78(2), June 2005: 287-304, http://onlinelibrary.wiley.com/doi/10.1348/096317905X26714/abstract.

9. Lawrence S. Krieger with Kennon M. Sheldon, "What Makes Lawyers Happy?: A Data-Driven Prescription to Redefine

Professional Success," *George Washington Law Review*, 83(2), February 2015: 554-627, http://www.gwlr.org/wp-content/uploads/2015/05/83-Geo-Wash-L-Rev-554.pdf.

10. Amy Adkins, "Employee Engagement in U.S. Stagnant in 2015," Gallup, January 13, 2016, http://www.gallup.com/poll/188144/employee-engagement-stagnant-2015.aspx.

11. Justin Berg, Jane E. Dutton, and Amy Wrzesniewski, "What Is Job Crafting and Why Does it Matter?" Center for Positive Organizational Scholarship, University of Michigan, August 1, 2008, https://www.researchgate.net/profile/Justin_Berg/publication/266094577_What_is_Job_Crafting_and_Why_Does_It_Matter_By/links/542a720d0cf27e39fa8e925c.pdf.

12. JK Boehm and LD Kubzansky, "The Heart's Content: The Association Between Positive Psychological Well-being and Cardiovascular Health," *Psychological* Bulletin, 138(4), 2012: 655-91, DOI: 10.1037/a0027448, https://www.ncbi.nlm.nih.gov/pubmed/22506752.

13. Ed Diener and Micaela Y. Chan, "Happy People Live Longer: Subjective Well-Being Contributes to Health and Longevity," *Applied Psychology: Health and Well-Being*, 3(1), 2011: 1-43, DOI:10.1111/j.1758-0854. 2010.01045.x, http://internal.psychology.illinois.edu/~ediener/Documents/Diener-Chan_2011.pdf.

14. "Optimism and Your Health," Harvard Men's Health Watch, Harvard Medical School, May 2008, http://www.health.harvard.edu/heart-health/optimism-and-your-health.

15. Laura A. Weiss, Gerben J. Westerhof, and Ernst T. Bohlmeijer, "Can We Increase Psychological Well-Being? The Effects of

Interventions on Psychological Well-Being: A Meta-Analysis of Randomized Controlled Trials," *PLOS One*, 11(6), June 21, 2016, DOI:10.1371/ journal.pone.0158092, http://journals.plos.org/ plosone/article?id=10.1371/journal.pone.0158092.

16. Martin E. P. Seligman, "Pleasure, Meaning & Eudaimonia," Authentic Happiness, University of Pennsylvania, 2002, https://www.authentichappiness.sas.upenn.edu/newsletters/ authentichappiness/pleasure.

17. David DiSalvo, "The Latest Science On Whether Money Can Buy Happiness," *Forbes*, February 28, 2015, http://www.forbes.com/ sites/daviddisalvo/2015/02/28/does-anyone-really-know-if-money-can-buy-happiness/#26d7e83c2512.

18. Alan S. Waterman, Seth J. Schwartz, and Regina Conti, "The Implications of Two Conceptions of Happiness (Hedonic Enjoyment and Eudaimonia) for the Understanding of Intrinsic Motivation," Journal of Happiness Studies, 9(1), 2006: 41-79, DOI: 10.1007/s10902-006-9020-7, http://link.springer.com/ article/10.1007/s10902-006-9020-7.

Chapter 3
How Your Hidden Biases Can Hurt Your Career

1. Richard M. Ingersoll, "Beginning Teacher Induction: What the Data Tell Us," *Education Week*, May 2012, http://www.edweek. org/ew/articles/2012/05/16/kappan_ingersoll.h31.html.

2. Bryant G. Garth, Robert L. Nelson, Ronit Dinovitzer, Gabriele Plickert, and Joyce Sterling, "After the JD III: Third Results from a National Study of Legal Careers," *The American Bar Foundation and the NALP Foundation for Law Career Research and Education,*

2014, http://www.americanbarfoundation.org/research/project/
44.

3.   James K. Harter, Frank L. Schmidt, Sangeeta Agrawal, Stephanie
      K. Plowman, "The Relationship Between Engagement at Work
      and Organizational Outcomes: 2012 12°Meta-Analysis," Gallup,
      February 2013, http://employeeengagement.com/wp-content/
      uploads/2013/04/2012-Q12-Meta-Analysis-Research-Paper.pdf.

4.   Patricia Chen, Phoebe C. Ellsworth, and Norbert Schwarz,
      "Finding a Fit or Developing It: Implicit Theories About
      Achieving Passion for Work," *Personality and Social Psychology
      Bulletin*, 41(10), July 31, 2015: 1411-1424, http://journals.
      sagepub.com/doi/abs/10.1177/0146167215596988.

5.   Martin Seligman, *Flourish: A Visionary New Understanding of
      Happiness and Well-Being*, New York, NY: Free Press, 2011.

6.   Amy Wrzesniewski and Jane E. Dutton, "Crafting a Job:
      Revisioning Employees as Active Crafters of Their Work,"
      Academy of Management Review, 26(2), April 1, 2001: 179-201,
      DOI:10.5465/AMR.2001.4378011, http://amr.aom.org/content/
      26/2/179.short.

Chapter 4
Got Mental Gremlins? Overcoming Negative Self-Talk

1.   Brené Brown, *Rising Strong: The Reckoning. The Rumble. The
      Revolution*, New York, NY, Spiegel and Grau, 2015.

2.   "Definition of disappointment in English," English Oxford Living
      Dictionaries. British & World English, 2017,
      https://en.oxforddictionaries.com/definition/disappointment.

3. Ray Williams, "CEO Failures: How On-Boarding Can Help," *Psychology Today*, May 2, 2010, https://www.psychologytoday.com/blog/ wired-success/201005/ceo-failures-how-boarding-can-help.

4. K Ann Renninger and Suzanne Hidi, *The Power of Interest for Motivation and Engagement*, New York, NY: Routledge, 2016.

5. Adam M. Grant. "Does Intrinsic Motivation Fuel the Prosocial Fire? Motivational Synergy in Predicting Persistence, Performance, and Productivity," *Journal of Applied Psychology*, 93(1), January 2008: 48-58, http://psycnet.apa.org/journals/apl/93/1/48/.

6. Chadrick Lane, "The Chemistry of Information Addiction," *Scientific American*, October 2009, https://www.scientificamerican.com/article/ are-we-addicted-to-inform/.

7. PR Goldin, M Ziv, H Jazaieri, K, Hahn, R Heimberg, and JJ Gross, "Impact of Cognitive Behavioral Therapy for Social Anxiety Disorder on the Neural Dynamics of Cognitive Reappraisal of Negative Self-beliefs: Randomized Clinical Trial," *JAMA Psychiatry*, 70(10), October 2013: 1048-1056, DOI: 10.1001/jamapsychiatry.2013.234, https://www.ncbi.nlm.nih.gov/pubmed/23945981.

8. Katja Gaschler, "The Power of the Pen," *Scientific American*, August 2007, https://www.scientificamerican.com/article/ the-power-of-the-pen/.

9. Karen A. Baikie and Kay Wilhelm, "Emotional and Physical Health Benefits of Expressive Writing," *Advances in Psychiatric Treatment*, 11(5), August 2005: 338-346, DOI: 10.1192/ apt.11.5.338, http://apt.rcpsych.org/content/11/5/338.full.

Chapter 5
Career Strength Training:
Making Your Work Better By Using What You Do Best

1. Alex M. Wood, P. Alex Linley, John Maltby, Todd B. Kashdan, and Robert Hurling, "Using Personal and Psychological Strengths Leads to Increases in Well-Being Over Time: A Longitudinal Study and the Development of the Strengths Use Questionnaire," *Personality and Individual Differences*, 50(1), January 2011: 15-19, DOI: http://dx.doi.org/10.1016/j.paid.2010.08.004, http://www.sciencedirect.com/science/article/pii/S0191886910003946.

2. Nansook Park, Christopher Peterson, and Martin EP Seligman, "Strengths of Character and Well-Being," *Journal of Social and Clinical Psychology*, 23(5), 2004: 603-619, http://www.viacharacter.org/blog/wp-content/uploads/2013/12/Character-strengths-well-being-Park-Peterson-Seligman-2004.pdf.

3. Shiri Lavy and Hadassah Littman-Ovadia, "My Better Self: Using Strengths at Work and Work Productivity, Organizational Citizenship Behavior, and Satisfaction," *Journal of Career Development*, February 2016: 1-15, DOI: 10.1177/0894845316634056, http://journals.sagepub.com/doi/pdf/10.1177/0894845316634056.

4. Laura Morgan Roberts, Gretchen Spreitzer, Jane E. Dutton, Robert E. Quinn, Emily Heaphy, Brianna Barker, "How to Play to Your Strengths," *Harvard Business Review*, 83(1), January 2005: 75-80, https://hbr.org/2005/01/how-to-play-to-your-strengths.

5. "The VIA Survey," VIA Institute on Character, 2017, http://www.viacharacter.org/www/Character-Strengths-Survey.

6. Jim Asplund, Shane J. Lopez, Tim Hodges, Jim Harter, "The Clifton StrengthsFinder® 2.0 Technical Report: Development and Validation," The Gallup Organization, February 2007, http://strengths.gallup.com/private/Resources/ CSFTechnicalReport031005.pdf.

7. Susan Sorenson, "How Employees' Strengths Make Your Company Stronger," Gallup, Inc., February 2014, http://www.gallup.com/businessjournal/167462/ employees-strengths-company-stronger.aspx.

8. Michelle McQuaid, "The 2015 Strengths @ Work Survey," VIA Institute on Character, 2015, https://s3.amazonaws.com/ showup-shine-succeed/The_2015_Strengths_At_Work_Survey- Michelle_McQuaid.pdf.

9. "How Employees' Strengths Make Your Company Stronger," Gallup, Inc.

Chapter 6
Examing Your Values: Seeking Purpose Every Day

1. Wayne F. Cascio, "Changes in Workers, Work, and Organizations," vol. 12, chap. 16 in *Handbook of Psychology*, ed. W. Borman, R. Klimoski, and D. Ilgen, New York: Wiley, 2003, DOI: 10.1002/0471264385.wei1216, https://www.researchgate.net/publication/ 228038525_Changes_in_Workers_Work_and_Organizations.

2. Catherine Bailey and Adrian Madden, "What Makes Work Meaningful—Or Meaningless," *MIT Sloan Management Review*, June 1, 2016. http://sloanreview.mit.edu/article/ what-makes-work-meaningful-or-meaningless/.

3. Justin M. Berg, Jane E. Dutton, and Amy Wrzesniewski, "Job Crafting and Meaningful Work," in *Purpose and Meaning in the Workplace*, ed. B. J. Dik, Z. S. Byrne, and M.F. Steger, Washington, DC: American Psychological Association, 2013: 81-104, http://justinmberg.com/berg-dutton--wrzesniewski_2.pdf.

4. Lilach Sagiv and Shalom H. Schwartz, "Value Priorities and Subjective Well-being: Direct Relations and Congruity Effects," *European Journal of Social Psychology*, 30(2), March 9 2000: 177-198, DOI: 10.1002/(SICI)1099-0992(200003/04)30:2<177:: AID-EJSP982>3.0.CO;2-Z, http://onlinelibrary.wiley.com/doi/ 10.1002/(SICI)1099-0992(200003/04)30:2%3C177::AID-EJSP982%3E3.0.CO;2-Z/abstract.

5. Geoffrey L. Cohen and David K. Sherman, "The Psychology of Change: Self-Affirmation and Social Psychological Intervention," *Annual Review of Psychology*, 65(1), January 2014: 333-371, DOI: 10.1146/annurev-psych-010213-115137, http://www.annualreviews.org/doi/abs/10.1146/ annurev-psych-010213-115137.

Chapter 7
Three Cheers For Negative Feelings at Work:
Using Emotions Strategically

1. Ulrike Malmendier and Geoffrey Tate, "Behavioral CEOs: The Role of Managerial Overconfidence," *Journal of Economic Perspectives*, 29(4), September 1, 2015: 37-60, DOI: https://doi.org/10.1257/jep.29.4.3, http://www.ingentaconnect. com/content/aea/jep/2015/00000029/00000004/art00003.

2. Andreas Kappes and Tali Sharot, "Optimism and Entrepreneurship: A Double-Edged Sword," Nesta, February 2015,

https://www.nesta.org.uk/sites/default/files/
optimism_and_entrepreneurship_-_a_double-edged_sword.pdf.

3.　Jennifer Kish Gephart, James R. Detert, Linda K. Trevino, and
Amy C. Edmondson. "Silenced by Fear: The Nature, Sources, and
Consequences of Fear at Work." *Research in Organizational
Behavior*, 29, 2009: 163-193, http://www.hbs.edu/faculty/
Pages/item.aspx?num=36259.

4.　"The Burden of Stress in America," NPR/Robert Wood Johnson
Foundation/Harvard School of Public Health, July 2014,
http://www.rwjf.org/content/dam/farm/reports/
surveys_and_polls/2014/rwjf414295.

5.　Karen Gasper, Regina H Lozinski, and Lavonia Smith LeBeau, "If
You Plan, Then You Can: How Reflection Helps Defensive
Pessimists Pursue Their Goals," *Motivation and Emotion*, 33(2),
2009: 203-216, DOI: 10.1007/s11031-009-9125-5,
http://link.springer.com/article/10.1007/s11031-009-9125-5.

6.　Alia J. Crum, Peter Salovey, and Shawn Achor, "Rethinking
Stress: the Role of Mindsets in Determining the Stress Response,"
Journal of Personality and Social Psychology, 104(4), 2013: 716-
733, DOI: 10.1037/a0031201, https://www.ncbi.nlm.nih.gov/
pubmed/23437923.

7.　Elizabeth D. Kirby, Sandra E. Muro, Wayne G. Sun, et al, "Acute
Stress Enhances Adult Rat Hippocampal Neurogenesis and
Activation of Newborn Neurons Via Secreted Astrocytic FGF2,"
eLife, 2(e00362): April 16, 2013, DOI: http://dx.doi.org/
10.7554/eLife.00362, https://elifesciences.org/content/2/e00362.

Chapter 8
Zeroing In On Your Career "Sweet Spot"

1.   Mihaly Csikszentmihalyi, *Flow: The Psychology of Optimal Experience*, New York: Harper & Row, 1990.

2.   Mihaly Csikszentmihalyi, *Creativity: The Psychology of Discovery and Invention,* New York, NY: HarperCollins, 1996.

Chapter 9
Mining Your Personal Resources to Boost Your Career

1.   "New Survey Reveals Extent, Impact of Information Overload on Workers; From Boston to Beijing, Professionals Feel Overwhelmed, Demoralized," LexisNexis, 2010, http://www.lexisnexis.com/en-us/about-us/media/press-release.page?id=128751276114739.

2.   Tony Schwartz and Christine Porath, "Why You Hate Work," *The New York Times*, June 6, 2014, https://www.nytimes.com/2014/06/01/opinion/sunday/why-you-hate-work.html?_r=0.

3.   K. Anders Ericsson, "The Influence of Experience and Deliberate Practice on the Development of Superior Expert Performance," Chapter 38 in *The Cambridge Handbook of Expertise and Expert Performance*, New York, NY: Cambridge University Press, 2006.

4.   K. Anders Ericsson, Ralf Th. Krampe, and Clemens Tesch-Romer, "The Role of Deliberate Practice in the Acquisition of Expert Performance," *Psychological Review*, 100(3), 1993: 363-406, doi.org/10.1037/0033-295X.100.3.363,

http://psycnet.apa.org/?&fa=main.doiLanding&doi=10.1037/
0033-295X.100.3.363.

5. Laura Vanderkam, "Stop Checking Your Emails Now," *Fortune*,
    October 2012, http://fortune.com/2012/10/08/
    stop-checking-your-email-now/.

6. Joe Robinson, "The Truth About Multi-Tasking: How Your
    Brain Processes Information," *Entrepreneur*, November 2012,
    https://www.entrepreneur.com/article/224943.

7. Martha E. Mangelsdorf, "What Makes Information Workers
    Productive," *MIT Sloan Management Review*, Winter 2008,
    http://sloanreview.mit.edu/article/
    what-makes-information-workers-productive/.

8. Candice L. Hogan, Jutta Mata, and Laura L. Carstensen, "Exercise
    Holds Immediate Benefits for Affect and Cognition in Younger
    and Older Adults," *Psychology and Aging*, 28(2), June 2013: 587-
    594, doi.org/10.1037/a0032634.

9. Barbara L. Fredrickson and Christine Branigan, "Positive
    Emotions Broaden the Scope of Attention and Thought-Action
    Repertoires," *Cognition and Emotion*, 19(3), 2005:313-332, DOI:
    10.1080/02699930441000238, https://www.ncbi.nlm.nih.gov/
    pmc/articles/PMC3156609/.

10. Michele M. Tugade and Barbara L. Fredrickson, "Resilient
    Individuals Use Positive Emotions to Bounce Back From Negative
    Emotional Experiences," *Journal of Personality and Social
    Psychology*. 86(2) 2004:320-333. DOI: 10.1037/0022-
    3514.86.2.320, https://www.ncbi.nlm.nih.gov/pmc/articles/
    PMC3132556/.

11. Marc G. Berman, John Jonides, and Stephen Kaplan, "The Cognitive Benefits of Interacting With Nature," *Psychological Science*, 19, 2008: 1207-1212, DOI: 10.1111/j.1467-9280.2008.02225.x, http://journals.sagepub.com/doi/abs/10.1111/j.1467-9280.2008.02225.x.

12. Shawn Achor and Michelle Gielan, "The Data-Driven Case for Vacation," *Harvard Business Review*, July 2015, https://hbr.org/2016/07/the-data-driven-case-for-vacation.

13. BB Gump, KA Matthews, "Are Vacations Good for Your Health? The 9-year Mortality Experience After the Multiple Risk Factor Intervention Trial," *Psychosomatic Medicine*, 62(5), 2000: 608-612, http://www.ncbi.nlm.nih.gov/pubmed/11020089.

14. Vatsal Chikani, Douglas Reding, Paul Gunderson, Catherine A. McCarty, "Vacations Improve Mental Health Among Rural Women: The Wisconsin Rural Women's Health Study. *WMJ*, 104(6), 2005: 20-23, https://www.ncbi.nlm.nih.gov/pubmed/16218311.

15. Zeidan, Fadel, et al. "Mindfulness Meditation Improves Cognition: Evidence of Brief Mental Training," *Consciousness and Cognition*, 19(2), 2010: 597-605.

16. Adrienne A. Taren, J. David Creswell, and Peter Gianaros, "Dispositional Mindfulness Co-Varies with Smaller Amygdala and Caudate Volumes in Community Adults," *PLoS One*, 8(5), May 22, 2013: e64574, DOI: http://dx.doi.org/10.1371/journal.pone.0064574, http://journals.plos.org/plosone/article?id=10.1371/journal.pone.0064574.

Chapter 10
Treating Failure Like a Scientist

1.   Andrea Vale, "Justice Ginsburg Gives Life to a Legend," *Scholastic*, University of Notre Dame, September 13, 2016, https://scholastic.nd.edu/issues/justice-ginsburg-gives-life-to-a-legend/.

2.   JK Rowling, "The Fringe Benefits of Failure, and the Importance of Imagination," *Harvard University Commencement*, June 5, 2008, http://harvardmagazine.com/2008/06/the-fringe-benefits-failure-the-importance-imagination.

3.   Melanie Stefan, "A CV of failures," *Nature*, November 1, 2010, http://www.nature.com/nature/journal/v468/n7322/full/nj7322-467a.html

4.   Melanie Stefan, "A CV of Failures."

5.   James W. Pennebaker PhD, *Opening Up by Writing It Down: How Expressive Writing Improves Health and Eases Emotional Pain.* New York, NY: Guilford Press, 2016.

6.   Angela L. Duckworth, Christopher Peterson, Michael D. Matthews, Dennis R. Kelly, "Grit: Perseverance and Passion for Long-term Goals," *Journal of Personality and Social Psychology*, 92(6), June 2007: 1087-1101, http://dx.doi.org/10.1037/0022-3514.92.6.1087.

7.   Drake Baer, "This Untranslatable Finnish Word Takes Perseverance to a Whole New Level," *Business Insider*, June 18, 2014, http://www.businessinsider.com.au/finnish-word-sisu-is-key-to-success-2014-6.

8.   Pema Chödrön, *Fail, Fail Again, Fail Better*, Boulder Colorado: Sounds True, 2015.

Chapter 11
Making It Happen and Sticking With It

1.   Roy F. Baumeister, Ellen Bratslavsky, Mark Muraven, and Dianne M. Tiee, "Ego Depletion: Is the Active Self a Limited Resource?" *Journal of Personality and Social Psychology*, 74(5), 1998: 1252-1265, https://faculty.washington.edu/jdb/345/345%20Articles/Baumeister%20et%20al.%20(1998).pdf.

2.   Kevin L. Rand, Allison D. Martin, and Amanda M. Shea, "Hope, But Not Optimism, Predicts Academic Performance of Law Students Beyond Previous Academic Achievement," *Journal of Research in Personality*, 45(6), December 2011: 683-686, DOI: http://dx.doi.org/10.1016/j.jrp.2011.08.004, http://www.sciencedirect.com/science/article/pii/S009265661100 1139.

3.   Peter M. Gollwitzer and Paschal Sheeran, "Implementation Intentions and Goal Achievement: A Meta-analysis of Effects and Processes," *Advances in Experimental Social Psychology*, 38, 2006: 69-119, DOI: http://dx.doi.org/10.1016/S0065-2601(06)38002-1, http://www.sciencedirect.com/science/article/pii/S0065260106380021.

4.   Edwin A. Locke and Gary P. Latham, "New Directions in Goal-Setting Theory," *Current Directions in Psychological Science*, 15(5), October 2006: 265-268, DOI: 10.1111/j.1467-8721.2006.00449.x, http://cdp.sagepub.com/content/15/5/265.short?rss=1&ssource=mfr.

5.   Edwin A. Locke and Gary P. Latham, "New Directions in Goal-Setting Theory."

6.   Lenny Bernstein, "It's a Week Into January and a Quarter of Us Have Already Abandoned Our New Year's Resolutions," *The Washington Post*, January 7, 2015, https://www.washingtonpost.com/news/to-your-health/wp/2015/01/07/its-january-7-and-a-quarter-of-us-have-already-abandoned-our-new-years-resolutions/?utm_term=.cac3e08a5eeb.

7.   Johanna Peetz and Anne E. Wilson, "The Post-Birthday World: Consequences of Temporal Landmarks for Temporal Self-Appraisal and Motivation," *Journal of Personality and Social Psychology*, 104(2), February 2013: 249-266, DOI: 10.1037/a0030477, http://www.ncbi.nlm.nih.gov/pubmed/23066883.

8.   Hengchen Dai, Katharine L. Milkman, and Jason Riis, "The Fresh Start Effect: Temporal Landmarks Motivate Aspirational Behavior," *Management Science*, June 23, 2014: 1-20, DOI: http://dx.doi.org/10.1287/mnsc.2014.1901, http://pubsonline.informs.org/doi/abs/10.1287/mnsc.2014.1901.

9.   Gabriele Oettingen, *Rethinking Positive Thinking: Inside the New Science of Motivation*, New York, NY: Current, 2015.

10.   Peter M. Gollwitzer and Paschal Sheeran, "Implementation Intentions and Goal Achievement: A Meta-analysis of Effects and Processes."

11.   Gabriele Oettingen and Bettina Schwörer, "Mind Wandering via Mental Contrasting as a Tool for Behavior Change," Frontiers in Psychology, 4, September 2, 2013: 562, DOI: 10.3389/

fpsyg.2013.00562, https://www.ncbi.nlm.nih.gov/pmc/articles/PMC3759023/.

12. Angela Lee Duckworth, Heidi Grant, Benjamin Loew, Gabriele Oettingen, and Peter M. Gollwitzer, "Self-regulation Strategies Improve Self-discipline in Adolescents: Benefits of Mental Contrasting and Implementation Intentions," *Educational Psychology*, 31(1), 2011: 17-26, DOI: http://dx.doi.org/10.1080/01443410.2010.506003, http://www.tandfonline.com/doi/abs/10.1080/01443410.2010.506003

13. Phillippa Lally, Cornelia J.M. Jaarsveld, Henry W. W. Potts, and Jane Wardle, "How Habits Are Formed: Modelling Habit Formation," *European Journal of Social Psychology*, 40(6), October 2010: 998-1009, DOI: 10.1002/ejsp.674, http://onlinelibrary.wiley.com/doi/10.1002/ejsp.674/abstract.

Made in the USA
Middletown, DE
01 July 2018